THE ANALOG BODY

THE COLLECTED POEMS
1984-2024
by Alexander Laurence

THE ANALOG BODY
by Alexander Laurence

Copyright © 2024 by Alexander Laurence
Published by Tofu Ink Arts Press. All rights reserved.
Edited by Brian L. Jacobs
Book design by JLTY Atelier

Front cover "Human" & back cover "Cosmo"
by Joseph T.Y. Lee

ISBN: 978-1-958661-02-4

Tofu Ink Arts Press, a celebratory venture, aims at publishing poems and other arts of un humdrum'd inclusive rhizomatic errant possibilities. We support polished work of established & emerging poets and artists that are absorbed in possibilities. We are committed to amplifying voices of the under-represented and marginalized. Art makes you think about thinking...

ABSORB POSSIBILITIES!

www.TOFUINK.com
A member of CLMP

This book is dedicated
to my family and all the friends we lost to Covid-19

CONTENTS

Book One: Early Poems (1984-1986)

Some of these poems appeared in Riprap,
The Union, Art/Life, and a very limited
chapbook called Denouements Sordides.

Book Two: The Brest Symphony (1986-1988)

Part of Brest Symphony was awarded The Ronald
Foote Award for poetry 1988 (CSULB).
"Masculine/Feminine" was from a longer work
co-written by Ann DeJarnett.
Most of the "Amsterdam Poems" were performed at
Safari Sams. "Are The Soldiers Licked" was
a performance reading with Ann DeJarnett on
Electric Violin.

Book Three: Words and Things (1988)

A shorter version of Words and Things was published in 1988, as part of the Ovundum Poetry Series.

Book Four: Genghis Khan's Daughter (1989)

Book Five: Alphabet Cities (1990)

Some of these poems appeared in The Bay Guardian, The Fold, Memo, Pearl Magazine and others. Some poems were read on the air at KUSF.

Book Six: Welcome To The Cabaret (1992)

Some of these poems were published in Talisman,
Pearl Magazine, Jejune, Memo, The Curse, and more.

Book Seven: One Corpse Said To Another (1998)

Book Eight: THE NEW SPAIN (2000-2020)

Some of these poems appeared in Blaze Vox, Acid Verses, and Sparkle + Blink 110 (Quiet Lightning).

Afterword:
THE ANALOG BODY:
THE COLLECTED POEMS
an introduction by Alexander Laurence

Book One: Early Poems (1984-1986)

ALL WOMEN MUST BE FATAL

Swinburne collapses in his mother's arms,
a bed of death, as his brother had done.
She watched her sons compassionately
without prayer, without speech: one to the sun,
one to the sea (only men are mortal).
Dark green is the sea, their mother. It is
the color of consumptive bile, the
color of her weak severe eyes. There, an epitaph reads:
"My author, the sun, it is up to you
that I've come my Father, I've expired."

MALIGN FIESTA

My gray nature is quickly aroused
Only during the blackest night or
A December full of funerals.
Is this really birth or death? Do I care?
I saw the wine being shared
Quietly among the sturdy
And wet faces. It was during
A bizarre meeting in Seal Beach.

In Spring, we will conceive
A truculent poison for all of our enemies,
And never speak a word of ill will.
In Winter, against the songs of mourning,
We have our own amour des feintes.
We will find our strengths
In each other's firm grip.
There is a black hole,
Where we used to find God.

When all future ceremonies
Have closed down and are far away
From one-sided memories.
And I am still in your bedroom

And sleeping in your moist bed.
You will then ask "Why will the flowers
We plant refuse to bloom?"
I remember seeing Orielle Wells
stealing a peach after school.
Don't ever think that there is an end
To love or longing.

There are not one, or two loves.
There are fifty loves.
Each one has a different face,
Different color, and different smell.

ALL THIS JAZZ

I hear all this jazz about phenomena
Lying on the doorstep with interest.
Holy mysticism impales sweet magic.
Everlasting misery, but swing it back to me.

It's a good day, but don't listen to me
Because I can swing in the sinister keys.
You are going to burn, burn with me.
We can feel the fire in third degrees.

All this jazz about King Oliver,
Jelly Roll Morton and Billie Holiday.
And all the downhearted, skag in vein.
Give me the blues fire, blues fire off once again.

Butter is bitter, but don't be a quitter.
Another sad song, the heart sinks asunder.
It's the blackening of the dark symphony.
People are deceitful, and still you believe?

It's all this damn jazz about love and hate.
Love of heroin, hate of withdrawals and misery.
I just want to feel your warmest embrace,
Not this empty feeling of being half-dead and lonely.

FOGGY MOUNTAIN BREAKDOWN

Soft petals are on the floor,
Brown rust and old dust,
Are very distant in my mind.
I am trapped in this prison.
My spirit naturally rebels
Against any harsh reality.

Many gates are closed behind me.
Now I am surrounded by the voices
Of damned souls and their circular memories.
If trapped in a collective misery, I choose
To retreat to some private backwoods.

I am also one of those strange monsters,
But a part of me is silently hidden.
The world is chaos, but in those quiet
Spaces is where I will find my future self.
I have never suffered from any payback.

A SPANISH LULL

The longest year ever was the year without music.
I hated those new songs, and even the old ones.
I slept for many nights without songs in my dreams.
Time is short, but a bad song seems to last forever.

I left the band, and have gone solo I guess.
I have so many records with Spanish guitar.
I listen to the New Wave radio station at
the coroner's office: I used to go to live gigs.

I drank for ages. That was preferable to a
Life with music and songs. Imagine the silent
Streets of yesteryear, and compare that to
Sounds coming out of every orifice possibly.

LANGUAGE

Can you return to that early day
Of last year by boat and train?
How many times must you return?

From the purple-lined country of
My ancestors, and even going back farther
To the odd fellows of the European countries.

To go back is to find old trinkets and ruins.
There are old men's stories and tales of dark love,
And we can trace ourselves back to the source.

These are dead words and impersonal discourse.
I never felt closer to nature despite all the words
and documents about expired lives.

All we have are these words and old documents.
I seek to live in the silence and places of
Inarticulation: no more words, but life!

THE FUNEREAL OF MAY'S FLOWERS

Can you let me see the hidden eyes?
Her unbridled beauty has been reduced by death.
A wreath and an unopened letter lie on the grave
Of this departed loved one who rots silently.

Yes, I did love this woman many years ago
in different circumstances and different times.
She was once so young and full of life; and now,
Still and restful, in a pose for all eternity.

We have one more drink as she sleeps beneath
This black and velvet city, as summer approaches.
My birthday passes, and all memories will pass too.
Where have the dead flowers gone to today?

LANGUAGE 4 (Nervous Spring)

I would like things to be different.
Mark the change in time, and each moment
Leads to the next. Imagine this new way!

But too often days seem the same and not different.
I am dealing with real life, and not grappling
with something vague and obscure.

I am not living without rules and lack of structure.
The rage for some order is not a search for truth.
When everything has been said, meaning emerges.

THE WINDOW-PANES

The window-panes hide the yellow fog.
The window-panes muzzle the bleak
Row of houses from any noise.
The window-panes can lick itself.
You don't have to question it.
I have a candle lit in the window
For someone.

I will return to those days
of decadence and soixante-neuf.
Along the white houses on
West Cromwell Road, I remembered
Lady Ottoline licked me.

The window-panes are indecisive.
The window-panes allow me to see
A drunk couple trying to have sex
From directly across the street.
These are the wonderful things in the world.
But if I read about them in a novel,
I wouldn't actually believe it.

CREDIT

I'll be there when someone arrives.
By now it is almost half past one.
My brief insanity caused me
To do it, but it was my intelligence
That allowed me to bring it off.
The arches pose for the camera,
Heads of cabbage, and other things
You received as Christmas presents.

We made a super 8mm film.
No journey; potentiality involves
The object which is subdued, not capable
Of movement, which performs this one
Gesture again and again till it is able to do
So by rote. I depend on that stability.

A VIEW FROM THE CAFE

We walked in from the alleyway
As we saw everybody stare at the floor.
I sat down at the nearest table
And the garçon came through the door.

Someone mentioned the weather.
A coin was dropped near a spoon.

You asked "Why did we come here?"
Then you smiled as if nothing happened.
I spilled my coffee once again.
I covered the mess with a napkin.

We're sitting in a haunted room.
Even the mirrors tell us to leave.

I favor a pint of plain right now,
But I imagine I have had too much today.

Have I really lived? There is no telling
When we are all sleeping in the grave.

We never existed.

THE ORANGE TREE 1985

As I look out this dirty window
I see the orange tree in the distance.
It is average and unremarkable.
Leaves struggle for air
Until they suffocate.
The stillness evokes something within me.
The orange tree produces fruit for years,
And sometimes oranges lie on the grass
And now they are rotten.
I am that tree.

INSIDE THE HOUSE

Somewhere leads to the hidden lights
and the relics of the distant past.
If I could be sincere and true, frankly
I could only confide to you, within these walls.

Within these walls is a timeworn mystery
Where my family have lived and died.
These secrets slip into an aging time,
As we journey further into the house.

I can see the shade, and can feel the solace
That may live beneath the house. I felt at home
And hid in the comfort for reasons unknown.
My death occurred inside the house.

Even on cold nights I stay outside now.
I will never go inside the house again.
I would rather beg for old pains and burn
A memory, ever since my expulsion.

A SPRINGTIME IN DOMINIQUE

Today I must insist that you recall that
One future day soon, that the fleuve of
The Laurence will freeze and flow no more.

Long sensual icicles with grow in
The chaos of poets' white beards
Across the black gothic underbelly.

And then, a blue-green day will come
To bring the warming airs of March
That fracture, and stir the waters of their beds.

Thick chills become liquid: ice cracks
And spills and emits fearful sobs and howls.
The Laurence wakes where it was dead.

And this is our music: not my words
Nor enchantments. All this will frighten
Your head into my chest.

And yes! Your soft body will enter into
The graveness of my embrace. For when
All else is borne, you will murmur to be ended.

For what else is there except to become
A poem forever of frigid winters?
You will never become flesh or a shifting river.

GHOSTLY SPIRITS 1981

I can see the end of the tunnel
In Chinatown. I have left my friends.
I haven't slept, and I can see morning light.
In the hotel room I can hear the furnace
But I am unable to sleep. The only congress
I know is the "progress of the crow."

I call a friend on the pay phone.
There is no answer.
It's the end of a weekend.
The previous night we were
at a punk rock gig at Mabuhay Garden.
Now I am crashing on alcohol
and drugs. Everyone loves
to feign these days.

Barbara didn't answer the phone either.
Soon I will get on a cheap PSA flight
and trip out of my mind all day.

A CIGARETTE AT 5:15

My fingers are dirty, brown, and inferior.
But that does not prevent me from
Lighting another cigarette as I walk
Past the hospital with its ill population.

I have so much on my mind, so much philosophy.
I have no time to think of insurance payments.
There is an inspiring fog in my lungs.
Babies have nothing but oblivion in their soft heads.
Spit, feces, urine, and endless trails of uncontrolled
Shit, do no honor to your lovely maddening eyes.
As I walk through this part of the hospital, it is
Like the part of the library that attracts the homeless.

Now my cigarette has gone out and I look for
the nearest ashtray: I see a man who has just died.
The life of a cigarette is no longer than any man's life.
A cigarette, or a man, should be no happier than me.

BAROQUE CURVE

At the narrow close of departure
In streets of discordance, a heart of acquiescence,
A quiet heart in the street's noisy air,
There is a nauseating quarrel of endless complaints.

His perplexed life begins to crawl there
Amid the turmoil, and amid the confusion.
And he had cried once or twice when he was young,
But on the whole, infrequently.

There is not an audience. A part of his life is a
Ghost of himself: his gaze into the past.
And when he lies, he lies on his back,
with his back to himself.

He can only be seen in the mirror.
He smiles when someone else looks at him, as if they
Really wanted to know all about him.
We close our eyes and shake our heads....

TWO GERMAN DANCES

Vulturing the lifeless in tombs
is a dirty business--only animals
will wake the dead.
Policemen and ex-soldiers
dealt cards and discovered
where lies a history of worms.

They re-arrived to this unmarked
place, remembered by a few.
(No one came here to pay respects).
They danced in an archaeology
of corpses, bones, mud, uprooting time.
They shattered the skulls
finding a fortune of gold
by cracking the teeth.

UNREAL CITY

I wish to move violently through walls
And find some unknown city where no one knows me.
I head towards the center of the city where the rain
And the purple fog greet me like familiar faces.

All I see are the eyes of strangers, walking by.
Is there one soul out there who can say
"Yes" to crime? All I can imagine now are
buildings on fire and screams into the vortex.

All these strange people are dead to me.
Is there one of you with the face
and eyes of the unforgettable Adrienne?
We could escape to the nearby woods.

UNE VIE TRISTE

My mind is spinning.
It's not very good for other things.
I feed on bread and tea, yet
Still, my lips feel dry and my
Back is sore, and I am out of toilet paper.

I missed school today.
The car accident wasn't planned,
but it was convenient for my friends.
I am looking for meaning
In the wrong places.

DEJEUNER LUGUBRE

No more mess with the bleeding eggs.
I would suck at the mouth of the uterus.
Vodka and boils, vodka and boils....
Shaving cream needed to shave today.
Shaving cream skin on the head.
Shaving cream: vodka and boils.

Dante stuck his buttocks in holy water.
Amsterdam was only a resting place.
Give Mister Solitaire some spare change.
Exchange rates: in strong monies.
Exchange rates: for poor black families.
Exchange rates: bon appetite, let's eat?

I was given reproduction advice again.
Screaming babies, smash the system.
They drove me to the house in Monte Carlo.
Horizontal: ideas of anarchy.
Horizontal: it's the year 1985.
Horizontal: the hole will be empty again.

THE GIANTESS
(for Gayle Hutchens)

She is reclined on a towering altar now
With perfumes and oils exuding from her body.
I do not speak out of turn in this silence.

When she walks, the world shall follow close:
Society is her tawdry playground and the men
She keeps, surround her like annoying flies.

I am also near her feet like a submissive cat.
The giantess is like a sphinx that confuses all.
My life and wants are alien to this temptress!

What the giantess thinks about is a mystery.
I live to be close to her somehow, and sometimes
I am unable to sleep. She could care less.

The giantess is the marriage of light and darkness.
There is the truth of pleasure and mortality, but
Never have I lived in the drowning light of love.

ERIK SATIE

Three Gilberts in the form of a pear.
A pear? Maybe an "M."
Is that any more believable?

You want form, you got it.
I think that I can hear Edith Piaf
In the background.

This annoyance is preventing
The next great poem.
Poets die, and artists continue to die.

Who is preventing this?
I know your answers already.
It's all "La Vie En Rose."

Satie died, and Piaf died.
And you say, "So what about Marilyn?"
You bastards!

HUSBAND AND WIFE

Sleep with knives and half-moons in meager beds;
Profligate and wordless. This clever year has passed.
It trudged along. A wind destroys: our garden is dry.
Only our blood, our creative powers, keeps us alive.
Our little world: is mouth to mouth as kindred spirits
Despite the calm noise of generations.

SUNDAY

Water blackened and heat rising
up the crystal pipes in time, slowly.
Men who walk in disturbing parks,
that you pass by, never know
the hour or the day, but you and I
sing to the dry fountains: I know
that there are many of those!
"Avec le rien de mystere, indispensable,
qui demeure, exprime, quelque peu."
Pigeons talk to each other
then fly away and evaporate
(fit for a princess, hot
on the heels of an angel).
I saw three that never came back.
I've seen gold on their backs.
All the same, he's never impressed
to know the program of the program -
the talk about economy in the papers.
I've never looked two ways when
crossing the street or when dreaming.
That is how I am when I walk on
deserted streets and when I am in love.
A palace opens at ten, but there
will be no one at home. I wonder
if anyone speaks French or Italian there?
All the birds that I've seen
couldn't fill that first room.
It is so quiet and dry.
My uncle is also locked in Portugal
with manuscripts and dollars.
I wonder if he can hear me speak?
Knowing him, it's possible! And I
remember now that he owes me twenty
dollars, and now my dear uncle,
I would like to buy some more bread.

Book Two: The Brest Symphony
(1986-1988)

CANTO I

And what could be made except sheer commentary
if not this which is itself, made, not a gaze into a river?
A nude reclines for portraiture. He saw the
moon in a river, and death; and he embraced it,
drowned. Does one need to describe things
as they are? Empty wind. Will that serve to change
your weather? Will the scent of a female cause you
to adjust your lenses and your eyes? Does one
ever know things as they are? Words glisten.
We admire the word that represents itself,
free in an order, but not exactly free, but as
if it became free in the disengagement as we
imagined it so. Things remain to be things. Words
words. Words show us something: perhaps
the shadow beyond the act of creation. And that
creation is an order outside all previous orders,
which could be a rare moment of reality.
"Poetry, ladies and gentlemen:
an expression of infinitude, an expression
of vain death and of mere Nothing."
Words become sounds, sounds that resound as music.
The rhythm of voices, and subtle music is all over
the earth: listen to it. Autumn words shed
their leaves. The primal voice named the things
of this world, and the word became the thing
spoken. Spoken yet already articulated by some
precept of language: premium, pregnant, and present.
The written law before speech or reality. Green
before brown -- the evening lands are fertile,
quiet, and blooming, Girls with arms full of roses.
From the start, language played a different music
separate from the world and its constant songs.
The word was never quite the thing we saw, although
it pretended to be -- we were all accomplices
to this image. We are all womb begotten, never
knowing where we came from, never remembering.
That first year, there were flowers in the windows,
and my family. My mother told me how "That

summer was the most beautiful summer, ever, and
not a worry at all." Many purple days in the park.
And that certain morning which I remember myself amid
the steel tables and the rude concrete. A hint of sunlight
beamed through the slits of glass, arranged in fours,
unlike any other sunlight which I have encountered, in
that, the logic of time was never present in this room.
Coffee brewed and breakfast is served, at midnight.
It is possible that we have to talk over these things
because they plague us. There were so many things which
I wanted to tell you, but I hadn't the time. And after a
year or two I did not see you that often to whisper.
Even the presentation of the same setting differs with time.
I remember tender moments of life, of glory, that took
place in the same area or space as other sufferings--and
if there is no time, and the past is now, we will always be
as husband and wife although we were never married.
How do you account for these disorders, Mr. Quinn? Has
night descended? Am I the cause of all these incongruities?
Does one need to describe things as they are?
Have you had a moment of sense in the last hour, Patrick?
Here, and only here, live all of my cancers.
A man wrote a composition of brilliant music for
an orchestra one day: a music that was written, notes
and words. A structure was built, notes were arranged
in beauty, and while sounds emerged from the
instruments, hidden beneath the audibility lived
an occult arithmetics. Music expressed a mirror of
freedom yet music was restricted by a certain measure.
All the freedom and the sublime that I admired
in songs seemed unbridled, but never was. Then I
understood the thing that was made, and the making.
Created music taught us to listen to the music
of the earth, the sacred sounds from the outside,
the air; they did not exist without being played by
some great orchestra, songs written by the great
composer. If they were not written, it was as if
someone wrote the score of this world. Everywhere
songs are breathing the silent winds, the children's choir,
and the organ grinder. All day we can hear the written

word of sacred songs by all the world in every language.
At night, the earth quiets in a long rest. Sleep wordlessly all.
And what could be made except sheer commentary
if not this which is itself, made, not a gaze into a river?
Wine is the soul of the earth and from the lips of God;
and that is why the taste is bitter. Le vin est l'âme
de la bête. Mon pere s'appelle le ciel. Ma mere Je
s'appelle le monde. Leur fils est une bête aussi; et
son sang s'écoule comme le vin. Wine from the lips of God:
a green ocean. Your oceans rustle and sway with
absinthe. My hair found its way to your heart, not your heart,
no never, but an image of your heart. A shattered wreck.
And lastly a word to a woman: I ask "how do you sleep?"
You have left scars all over my body and recline in your
propitious innocence. With you, the past is what you mold
it into! Our Protean age! And you say that you have no use
for fictions! You are the best example of the perfect fiction,
although you have misunderstood them all: yours and mine.
You must choose at this moment to sign your books or
not. The hours are over so soon. Do you fear these words
as well? Do you fear yourself? Can I join you in the fear?

CANTO II

But no man shall see the garden, ever;
verses born in Venice sleep and die
there -- homage we may bestow someday
as if it was the day that Helen of Troy
appeared. They put the seer into a cage as they
would an animal, without woman or muse.
And you saw her too; a sound would
not be heard as sound, not only as sound,
but something else, riveder le stelle:
vision and sound. The breast of
the Mediterranean I saw, but I was
stranded with sight alone in
that moment; waiting to be there,
but never there. Both always there,

and wanting to be. Withdrawing.
If sight alone separates, one can
choose from being without sight
or being a man. "The garden returns"
in the imagination, and there alone,
we hope, a possibility that man
could not be only one or the other,
but sovereign of both: that man could
have blindness and sight in an instant,
a wounded man, and a Cyclops in the south.
I hear the seer explain those butchers in the streets
of New York, the detritus of culture.
He threw a book up in the sky,
the wind ignored it, as a child.
He was naive. He did not know
that those birds could not read,
that was 1938 or thereabouts.
I remember Barbara, how she was,
not in the photographs, back
when men drank beer and knew
nothing about the war. The last one
was nearly forgotten. I was devouring
biscuits and warm butter and sticky jam.
She dreams of stillborn infants,
later to appear in the paintings
of Goya. The trees swayed in a calm
temperament though I detected a villain
in those pages of history.
Who wrote the dictionary of the world?
Did he include the words "brutality"
and "forgiveness?" Who won the dice roll?
He who later became the professor
at the university. I remember the blue
of the sky without symbols, the utter emptiness,
and that alone made me want to paint,
to mix colors and words. Barbara was a young girl
back then whom I should have married, but I was
given a train ticket. I ate a big breakfast,
and wrote letters for many years.
This is the family scrapbook. In here

are fragments of fragments that have been
ignored, forgotten or left behind, and it is
times like these that we must crack open
its shell. Nostalgia. All the ruins and lies
of the past, stuff my mind does not want,
the graveyard of meaning. There is a big cloud
passing by, and it is a dark day. We shake hands
briefly and say so little. And it was as if
I had just talked with you yesterday, but it has
been four years; perhaps all that time has
disappeared suddenly, and not that much has
occurred. An old lady stares out the window
on the third floor. Death has lived here since
the beginning. My grandmother and your
grandmother are waiting and do not understand,
and do not want to. A disappearance, our fathers
who are not there anymore. Vague memories
of their faces. I do not think that he will
return. I came here because I thought I would
find you here, within these old pages.
Brothers and sisters will leave both of us
one day, family gone, and it is difficult to see
one another frequently. And when one sees
them again, they are so difficult, speech is
often difficult with time. But some treat you
as if you had never left, and then who are you really?
I hate that! Things have occurred, and
there is something changed in me. Old friends
unfasten themselves from one's life, and one
rarely hears from them, more pass away.
Images of my mother: a cinema,
photographic, and a show of films.
A passing of time in the present.
What I can see is the old mother
before me, and recollections
of some prehistory that I do not know.
Remember those who asked "should
Pound be executed for insulting the
economy, and giving us the Italian
and the Chinese in a fair exchange?"

The sublime word replaces the whore.
Francesco Clemente, a dilettante of sorts,
knew her well, saw her often though
cannot speak as the rain does
beating in the mud "Étoile du ciel!
mais rire, ma folie vous revelé
et ma mort vous rejoindra."

CANTO III

Foliage arabesque in Brest,
and my father dead.
Cups from the kitchen on the table.
Flamenco in the afternoon,
that morning a harpsichord:
a romance, a ruffiano!
Dry leaves left for us to sweep,
ah, what a task! Over green
and white; and green and brown.
He was left-handed, but played
the Mandolin. He knew the signatures.
Read the works of the masters.
I do not remember sometimes, and that
allows me to pause and seize the past
as if the past was locked, or placed,
in my brain in anticipation of surgery.
Yet what then is forgotten?
Hands that produce fish after fish?
Never had a year been so vacuous though
at the same time I instilled the
impression in myself that I had
done quite a lot on the other hand.
I did not kiss you. I have in the past.
But I am not one to tell all about it, .
record it here, as if this is a point
of rest. Encumbered by a past, most
would thrust it aside as if it did not
exist, hasten its disappearance. We

always tell ourselves that there is
the future to redeem ourselves, to fall,
to make the same mistakes. Is that any
hope, or is that a thing to look forward
to? In the future there are several blank
pages waiting to be filled, the sun
returns yet again as if we were counting.
Another day is due. But tomorrow is
death. I am writing my autobiography
on a mirror whilst the trees ignore
my gestures. It rained again today.
I walked for a few miles in the city
without an umbrella. I had a hole in
my right shoe; it was a crack that leaked.
"Where babes suck, there suck I"
said Shakespeare. I live by such mottoes
and white is the color of Shakespearean roses.
So tell me guitar player, does music
belong to you or to the guitar? It must
belong to neither since there would not
be a song without a guitar or a player.
The strings strain: they tell me that music
makes itself and belongs to every ear.
It was only a recording, not itself,
not the actual music of a harpsichord--
only an image of its voice.
Nothing is such a potential mnemonic
as music: a phrase that had changed
you or I, and the joyous remembrance of it.
Quiet noise, and the people who pass.
Tarpaulin, oil, and wax. I sit silently
to rest. Children drawing pictures on
paper, knees on the floor. Old women gazing.
These things I am here to see. Surface
and texture. Three-dimensional, words.
Diaspora. Heavy materials on canvas
and the violent profusion of languages.
Then the noise of shoes walking
across on wooden floors. Daylight and
soft sounds. To those who cannot enjoy.

Those who cannot play in the theater of sense.
An old man died in the flood, and
a few days before I recall that I
saw him throwing dice. I could never
get his name right when I was younger.
The last few times that I visited him,
he reminded me of this to my shame.
The ease of machines that go one way,
they have no problems nor decisions.
They do not know that even chaos has
its own harmony. The tempo and meter
of chance becomes the opposite of what
we thought was nonsense. Machines sound
off "fortissimo" at regular intervals,
they want to make sense. Through
repetition we then see the beauty of
the image or whatever. To destroy
the image, to break it up into pieces,
does not retell the ghost of truth.
One must continue to destroy to get
the right sound, the right image,
the right word. Power is so attractive.
Where does it come from?
I used to like you when
you did not know. Knowledge lives at the
expense of ignorance. Knowledge is power
only if it is hidden. Yesterday I read the
history of our victories -- I learned of
a civilization and the heroes. The absence
of a center, of truth, will allow power
to change its direction from time to time.

CANTO VI

"I don't have to go to the Arctic
to know it's cold" I panic
at morning, crack of ice and water,
Hear, hear the music there
in the sun and wind over water.

Not one bird this time of year,
no, never. Neither a feather.
Music brings me across
the violent sea. Across the
way my pale star, under the
mist, or in a great void; and
I move towards some great
limit. The chest at first, and
then the lungs inhale as do beat
the massive sails of a ship.

I climb the backs of all
the mountainous waves, and
the night enshrouds me.
I lie in the hull of the boat.
I feel vibrating in me all
the passions and thoughts
of a boat that badly suffers;
the kind wind, the quick tempests,
and their shifting convulsions
on the immense abyss. All three
lull me to sleep; other times,
the dead calm of the large glass,
a mirror, and my despairs.

When I was young, I wrote such
stories, and read when my fears
showed and I could not sleep.
Did you ever see the haunts
of whiteness? All the nights
a fire in the furnace: embers,
smoke, then soot. It is

a moment before sleep,
a moment before death.

Memories of the fish, out
of the water, on dry lands
to be bought and sold. Fished
them out of the canal, early.
In the fish-market, only
a dead man will swim.

In lines, ear to ear, frozen
slightly, you saw the first chaos
of the sun, and an old woman singing:
"one, two, three... that will
cost you two-fifty"

Over the fire, the dinner is ready.
Murderers. All the family well-fed
through war-time, through slaughters
and a score of winters.

I am only a young lad who prefers
fish to fowl. I sleep in a white blanket
of snow: a polar bear.

"The future can only be anticipated
in the form of an absolute danger."
We live as others have reconstituted
our world, rather than creating our
meals from naught, raw and cooked.

At the end of the land, the boats
depart from the wharf. The white smoke
of burning fires mixes through the crowd,
fish devours fish. There shall be more
for your children's children, you think.

Hunger makes you blind and lustfully weak, and
no shadows are allowed by sight, no
chiaroscuro. I feel that I am staring at

the blank page which cannot be written on
or the last blank page after a book ends.

CANTO IX

Savoy Tifoli, and my childhood near the window.
    Quinn points and tells the story again, Mr. Paul Cuadra
        listens, I can remember Lou Dansky from years ago.

None of them ever enjoyed this view that I possess.
    Tequila and cigarettes, beers and friends,
        women and the sunlight. Music from inside.

A breeze through here, a wind. I showed everyone
    my photographs. People, French and German. There is
        a familiar woman, her hair, her face.

North Beach! Up there Mister! Up there! you told the
    cabdriver in '77. Lemon and orange houses, still from
        from the sixties, buildings, Italian restaurants.

A cup of coffee on Telegraph Hill: espresso, cappuccino,
    cafe latte. They tell me Richard Brautigan lived here, a block
        away from my neighborhood. Never saw him. Others

lived here as well. Where are Quinn and Malacoda? We all
    lived here and were friends. Shared a room. In the summer,
        warm airs and the memory of cruelty. The cruelty

of memory. I been writing letters every day now, in search
    of those lost friends. Look around. The Chinese, no rivers
        down this street, a bay near (silence is not a word).

Maurice Blanchot is ignored this year, no radix this year, totum
    malorum. Radix need not pronounce itself, it is written
        on the sky. Dismiss the universities! Logos dismantled!

Dismiss commentary, political writings, dismiss! The only thing
said is the method. All we have are interpretations. Awake!
Awake! From some back page I read "sleepers awake!"

Gilbert Sorrentino in Palo Altos, author in his dark room.
In the closet, creating beauty like no
one alive today, a rose theater, beauty alone.

Writers write in that moment, and not again,
practicing their capacity of not writing. Where
dark trees once were, an inner light exudes

for an instant; but we only remember the precise
instance of the lightning flash rather than the blackness
of the silent night. The last word was written in

the book, and the book was cast into the lives of the many,
the plural: many thought many things when the author was
making napkins. I bought a novel by someone whom

I never knew, and I walked through my old neighborhood with
nothing on my mind. I am full of anticipation when no one
is looking. Sculptors would make full symphonies

out of the wind, made calculations, and utilized arithmetic.
And structures that were not there before evolved like all
art ever was to be. The insignia was engraved on

the first page, and then I noticed how a series of images and
words attacked me in a brilliant succession, as if I had
arrived in Jupiter. Write to me, sometime.

Letters back home to my girlfriend remain unmailed, stagnate.
She enjoys herself, is by herself, controls the knowledge
of herself. The way of knowing, a forced reading.

We will never speak to each other again. It is no use. Letters.
Of seeing, of seeing, of knowing, she will no longer let
myself see, I will never know the truth -- Blind.

Another beer, North Beach. A bliss, a sublime bliss that cannot
        be had anywhere else. The weather. Dogs on the sidewalk.
            Old men in the Mission district do not interest me.

They are not beautiful, but perhaps were, some yesterday. This
        day is becoming old. I tried to find a few friends last night.
            Called them. Kel lee Cannis is gone: New York.

Now night had come on, rough, with no moon, but a nightlong
        downpour setting in, the rain-wind blowing hard from
            the west. Damn the elements! Stand under covering

watching the day end in this dampness. This is not a river,
        though I thought of you in this chaotic moment, to be
            caught dead, floating in the pulsating waves.

Adagio diminuendo. This is not a river of someone's tears.
        I could care less about the slipperiness under my feet,
            the danger of cold death: the abandonment of

the moment. And if death is near, come here and let's have
        it over with. Let me see what else there is, if there
            is anything? And only if it is final and real.

I want to fade into a fist of water, as if it was all some
        great curse. Rainwater against my skin and from my face
            and lips I remove the moisture. I wipe it all away.

And in that distance I see the rain beating on the pavement,
        the street of noises, and I listen. This is not a river, but
            perhaps it is music. In those sounds, those notes,

those instruments, I lose myself in their swirling winds --
        and as if I tried to stop thinking, to forget to think,
            to slip into the absence of thinking, of thought, to sink

into the void of language and sound.

CANTO X

Music in the streets, of hammer, of fingers, of voices.
Singers in a bar. A black man and a trumpet. Violin
there still around this corner. And there are workers

creating new buildings, metal beams, one nearly died.
Truck driver, cars in traffic, the radio: San Francisco.
Haight street, North Beach, Downtown, Mission street.

My brothers lurk somewhere in these streets, and me,
I am always trying to remember, and trying to remember
has made me numb to the past. I hardly recognize my past.

Michael Angelo Torres. We went out Monday night and I
do not know where you are. I wait for you, and listen
to the night's voices and the cars which pass overhead.

Guitars play, voices sing, they talk, they talk and sing.
And the moon nowhere, no more faces, the only violence
is the rain, the sky is thick with clouds. Moving briefly.

When all this ends it must be said. He said: "when a book
dies, it does not die as a bird, but with its wings spread"
A vanishing book, and a bird, or a man, a dying man.

"A structure of words, and then death" he prescribed.
"Words sing their swan song, they sing as they are written"
You haven't read a book unless you have been an accomplice

to a murder. "Aletheia" was the word written on the wall.
"A forgetting, a reading, writing to forget" Surrounded by
vague figures and unfamiliar names, I continue to walk.

"One cannot forget, unless they write the word" The elders
saw this perfectly, the scribes. "Then all is healthy: reading,
writing, and memory" Characters on walls, unsigned.

"Les lettres du blanc...." Are they written by a white man, an Anglo-Saxon? White letters? For whom? Quiet evening. Harmonie du soir, ce soir. When the time comes....

And jealousy? Is there jealousy? No jealousy, but fondness of the absence, that I could not conceive of before. Only death can take the place of my absence, your absence.

But her absence? I can remember that moment in which I tried to arrest the moment, to discontinue time, to bring myself some continuity, to quit, to look at you....

Permanent gaze: Orpheus possibilities, impossible sex. And then the time when the truth is no longer important. We can take pleasure in the mystery, and let the mystery stay.

The command becomes the order, a demand for an order, any order, where there is no order. An unknown richness from an extreme poverty. Violence and the sacred.

Excerpt From Masculine/Feminine
A book with Ann De Jarnette

SONG ONE

Have you ever lived?
Never there. Never here.
Always loved to.
There she is.
There he is.
When I fell down the stairs
I plunged toward my treasure.
Every dog will climb a tree
if some cat is there.
There was a nasty verb involved.
What does love want with me?

SONG TWO

I will come to you in the nighttime.
The sweet array of faithless birds.
You did not bring the expensive violin.
The graveyard sings: the dead will dance.
Let all time go: rise above space and time.
Summer: you left for Europe without me.
Our kiss is a revolt against mortality.
We drink to the downfall of lovers.

SONG THREE

My golden-hair has departed.
She has gone to the devil's acre.
I remember your heavy touch.
We lived and we drank together.
The palate of my strange tongue still burns.

Your hips would be handy in a rowboat.
Some black shape in my heart remains.
At some point you have to choose
Either self-love or object-love.
I will choose "The New Spain."

A LIFE IN AMSTERDAM

There are twenty-six figures
Near the promising tracks.
The train comes in
Plaguing all with euphoria.

When life is new,
It moves in the light.
When life is in decay,
It sleeps by the backdoor.

One more visit to the whorehouse
Will not resolve the price of life.
Several trains come in the station,
From each direction, causing confusion.

To walk on those insane streets
And feeling the blood in the veins.
The human form is first assumed,
Then collides and falls.

If one must be, it may become
Just a stain on the sidewalk.
This city changes, and we all walk by
And see all the previous marks.

THE SINGER IN THE STREET

An organ grinds
A depressed mood.
His monkey clutches
The cash for food.

Two beggars dance
And expect the same.
They have no talent
But one leg is lame.

A young Italian sings
His own Don Juan.
His spirit is sad,
His loved one is gone.

These facades are dismal.
My bereaved band
Laments and repents.
If alive, so they can.

THE BLACK SHEEP GIRL
(for Monica Welle)

Hearing other's stories is a life's duty.
So gather round the fire, and listen
To the tale of the black sheep girl.
Each passing word is so important,
the girl is furtive and strange.
I hear the distant sounds of an organ
and the celebration of the holidays.
Her family is downstairs near
a glaring Christmas tree.
All blackish green and golden light,
I see my girl in the mirror.
I am lying down in bed and the birds
Outside sound like they are speaking Greek.

The family itself were at least five or six.
Her dad had three daughters, and all his
Long life he wished for a son.
Fornication is a sin, or so it is said.
If you are going to sin, you could
At least get what you pray for?
Another year passes, and Christmas
Comes, and he is reminded of this past sin.
"I wanted a son all my life!" he said.
All I get are these girls, who he
doesn't really understand. Being the third
One: she started calling herself
"The Black Sheep Girl."
She always felt lonely, until she grew up
And left her small hometown one day.

A VIOLIN

Propped against a slender neck.
Waiting for the bitter note,
and the elevation of the last
Passionate sound in the room.

Like waiting from the drops emptying
Out of a terrified glass till drained
Of all breath and inspiration.
There is a time and an age.

Let us look forward to that day
When you are renewed and reborn.
I cheer on the upcoming flood
Of the heroic songs of a violin.

THE ANDALUSIAN GIRL

The girl sits in an open field
and she has flowers in her hair.
She also has a basket full of flowers.
A man looked on, as men often do.

She thought of all those years behind her.
And there were so many years in the future.
She thought about these thoughts often,
because that was all she ever thought about.

Once particulars are given, we can move on
to the whole, which can never be
quite "the whole" ever. Just like those notes
of music which may stand apart from the rest.

You drove to Vermont in the winter, towards
the end, and you found that she had greatly aged.
Your memory is so immense. Then going from one
room to another in life, and thinking it will be someone
else and not her who will eventually grow old.
Fretfully she will paddle out of the morass,
the thick advancing trouble we are in.
And the days roll by as you do.
This book may very well be, at the end of the day,
a rather large boat will drift off into the ocean.
It will sink and become a lost city.
Off in the distance, I hear what sounds like an oboe
that has caught my attention.
A large gray antelope walks through
a field, on television,
and yet you bore a son.

The little girl becomes a little man
struggling with the weight of things.
It is only her who knows what the hell
is going on in life.
She is so intelligent.
Is there only one language and one sex?

It was not bad, and he wrote out a
check for all the expenses.
A surging voice interrupts whatever
we were talking about that day.
You had mentioned some vague notion about
something called polarography.
I didn't understand what you were
talking about.
He fell into a hazel tree accidentally,
during a pause, and she therefore became
convinced of his sincerity; although at the
same time, I wanted to bring in a guillotine.
What is her maiden name? And why
is her name no different now?
They took one look at us and asked:
"Are you qualified for experimental testing?"
I am game at the beginning, but after the money
came in, I was off to the East Coast.
The garden was spurred on by water and manure.
It was often hindered by tholeiites.
When she was known to recruit husbands
in September, and they were soon put out to pasture.

THE WHORE EARTH

The fruits of the earth are feeding
the children and they are bored.
Every morning it's the earth and sky.
Somehow I figured out where I was
when I woke up.
In the newspaper there was a story
about a multiple birth.
I went down to a cafe near my house
and ate breakfast.
I sat outside near the door in the shade.

There was something remaining from last night.
Apparently during sleep I was shouting

for someone to stop. It was a horrific feeling.
The dogshit is all over the sidewalks.
No more chasing castles that don't exist.

I took a bus and met you on the other
side of the city. We met at a bar, and
the drinking continued. Something
always lingers from the past.
There are always new places that
I would like to visit.
The cold and the rain
contribute to the eventual decision.
All the smells and the warmth
coming from elsewhere, and every corner.
It gets late and I have to go home.

SHOOTING DOWN SUBMARINES

This notice to appear,
I write for you,
but obviously you can
plan to fail.

There are other things
to waste time and energy on.
Why must I pay you
with cash?

There are people who
never smile.
Why weren't we invited
to the art opening?

Something smells fishy.
I hate having enemies.
I feel like I'm holding a hammer,
and everything looks like a nail.

POMP AND CIRCUMSTANCES

Near voices like the trees.
A brilliant apple, and you ate it.
I walked over the unused
train-tracks quickly.
I became estranged to news.
I know of people who cannot
count certain amounts.
Is this my future as well?
There are roses that are never sold.
I ignored his irritating habits.
I apologized for road rage.
Then later with an eraser,
most of it went away.

I DO NOT SMOKE

No! It was not me.
I did not say those words
three years ago.
It must be your imagination.
But when we walked in the room
and sat down at the table:
minutes later, everyone left, and
left us with the bill.

At least I received a free book.
I drove past that club that you
recommended. The name was interesting.
When I came back another time
it was already closed. The room
was full again that night.
We discussed things like Freud
and school, but it was all off the mark.
My excitement has dissipated.
There could be new rooms to rent,
new friends in letters. With luck,

there will be no cheap seats,
no bones, and no more waiting.

Possibly it is that you
let me down and forgot me.
You grew up in Portsmouth
and bought a ticket to America.
There were a few exciting years
followed by boredom.
You are not missing out on anything,
and you have kids now.
Now that I think of it,
I will have a cigarette.

THE WINTER JOURNEY

It's the end of the winter journey.
It feels like the end.
Leaving it was impossible.
I only embarked because
I wanted to see you again.
I received your message
but read it incorrectly.
I didn't know what to think,
and was unable to read
between the lines.

Dear anyone:
I can feel you sitting
near me at Cafe Trieste.
Do you ever wonder
what Samuel Beckett meant?
Let's talk soon after the play.

The ladies were in the room,
with musicians and iced drinks.
I did not want to go there.

I don't think that I was invited.
Shall we go somewhere else?
A friend called me today:
he said that he was hit by a car,
and could not call me for a
few days. Having been at hospital.

Pier 39: holidays and subtle
movement of faces. The lark:
its brown quickness eludes me.
I remember the ferry boat
to Sausalito: even though I felt ill,
the trip felt like a revolution.

The cold surrounds me at night.
There is a dark cloud of rain.
My eyes are unable to penetrate
this dark wet night.

I am looking for something.
It's all constant motion.
Night can become no darker.
Night cannot be colder.

DESCRIPTION OF A PHYSICAL STATE: FERDINANDO GALIANI AND DIALOGUES SUR LE COMMERCE DES BLES

Call it that! The gentle joints which
crack when called upon to perform; and the mind
(Attempting to adapt to the environment
with no success) is drunk and dizzy rather than
talkative. Do not forget that one must
thank one's friends for the advice. After
all the rum cordials and the clams, one
must recollect: Je laisse a Gavarni. Poete des
chloroses, son troupeau gazouillant de
beaute d'hopital. And my woman is far away
to this day I have not met her; but listen
to the words of others' conversations, unless they want
you to listen—Mais Ecoutons! Chacun a son
gout! Out of context, words seem truer....

My Saint John Perse, and not yours. I mean
that is how I read him: and every morning I
stare at my barren bankbook and all my long
receipts—all everyone needs is receipts! But
once I saw in a museum on the same wall
the works of both Claude Monet and Rene Magritte.
What a shame! I dipped another wafer
into a cup of stale tea: time has passed!
Quelle dommage! I become lost in paintings.
Look at that portrait of Monsieur Galiani:
it is impressive to only me and no other.
I often wonder what was behind those eyes?
But I will never know anything about this man,
so obscure, and so out of time, and it is no matter!

THE CELEBRATION

Let this all take place in the apartment of Algernon Malacoda, also known as Malacoda, and Pierre Blanche, also known as Peto, in the Latin Quarter.

It happened in this small apartment on the seventh floor. Malacoda was let in by Mahu, his neighbor. Mahu was a fighter. He was the biggest guy on the block. He was a tough guy. Peto, who is also know as Pierre, was sitting in a chair near the window where he was smoking cigarettes. Such was the life of a thief. Malacoda turned on the heat. He was a teacher. He was a professor of literature. In the room where most of us where sitting, was a large bookcase which gave the impression of being in a library. Oh yes! I was there too. We were all waiting for Minette to arrive in Paris that day. She was an American model who I met in London the previous year. She had returned to California, due to the death of her brother. She was due back. None of us thought of meeting her at the airport. She said "Don't worry about me!" I did not have an idea where she was.

Mahu left the apartment to retrieve something. He came back later with a box of tea and some other things. Malacoda took all this stuff from him and put it away. Mahu had big hands. Peto was reading a book. I opened the curtains to look out the window. An extreme amount of light came in.
The water boiled then. Mahu went to the bathroom. Malacoda ate a slice of bread with butter on it. He was reading Proust that day. I soon drank some wine. A toilet flushed. Malacoda brought in a pot of tea to the central table. Peto coughed loudly. Malacoda compared the girth of the teapot to Dante's head. Mahu sat down. I looked at his arms which looked like he experienced hard labor in the past. A thin layer of smoke hung in air. We were all waiting. There were bottles of alcohol and presents.

Malacoda took some photographs of us all. I took one of him. Peto had drained his cup and poured another. Malacoda insulted some person I didn't know. I stood up, and went to the bathroom. I needed to shave. Mahu turned on the radio. Peto was reading again. I think it was some recent book in German. I spread lather all over my face. We were still waiting for some guests.

MONTREAL, QUEBEC AND BELGIUM

I am mixing around in the chloroform streets.
I am high on books and knowledge, and walking
from end to end of the city. I am not sure if I am
following some stranger or becoming mad.
Sometimes I feel like throwing myself in the river.
But I have already lost some many good friends
these past two years, it's like there is some great war
going on that I don't know about. Previous girlfriends
have ignored me for ages, or could be dead now?
The tacky summer has arrived, and all the colorful
tourists have taken over every town. I am still feeling
like it's the first day of spring and full of passions.
Talking to anyone would be like talking to a clam
deep in the black sand. Why am I so out of touch with
this age? I feel like I have been asleep for a thousand
years and woken up by some sea captain or other.

I am not the enemy but everywhere I go dogs bark at me
and children try to kick me: I get all the unwanted attention.
For some reason, all my true friends went on holiday and
didn't warn me, and left me alone in this strange city.
I have resorted to live among old saints and gothic buildings
and follow any feeling that has a sense of mystery.
I look forward to that distant day when I can enjoy
the company of familiar eyes.

ANOTHER DEATH OF MONSIEUR UNTEL

The lamplights and the view are fixed.
Of some scene, of some view.
There is a man in the play of things.
From a box, a bird is green divided by blue.

Of some room, in some distinct age.
The chairs are neatly tucked, every shirt
is pressed. In some room of some view.
One must be precise of all the dirt.

There is not a man in the box, but a bird
that is silent because nothing moves or sings.
I look at the room once again: I notice
that the room is involved in the play of things.

But enough of this silly room and enough of this man.
Enough of this box! And the chairs and the lights!
Of some view, of some scene. In some room
the view is fixed of all the nights.

PAGAN CIRCLE

Spring will open each of her arms
to the first light upon the earth.
The feast of ages is blooming
as an unseen recurring birth.

And dreams of the vast evergreen
with the sacred promise it yields.
Requiring rhythmic offers
to soak in the musical fields.

Carried and impassioned in movements
between fertile ground and youth.
Nature is love: let a virgin come
forth and strengthen this truth.

To dance till exhausted of life,
her spirit cleansed by our deathly songs.
Return to the earth, go there young child!
Where once born, where the body belongs.

ARE THE SOLDIERS LICKED BY THE OLD FRIEND OF MAN, BECAUSE I HAVE SEEN THE DRIED BLOOD?

(Malacoda and Peto have gone to Iceland)

I am the frozen sensuality with the sublime
instruments of industry behind me. I am not
a fisher king contemplating sea animals, but
an exile trying to keep warm by dancing on
sidewalks and trying to sing the new song
of the next century. We neglect the dream of Spain.

I walk past suits and trenchcoats with newspapers.
They surely won't read that nonsense, will they?
Peto is sitting alone in some restaurant somewhere.
Probably next to fat old ladies with dyed hair.
For lunch, they eat bagels and crabs quickly.

I smell something distinctly yellowish.
It smells like some coward on a boat.
Any scrap of food will be pounced on
by some bird or nearby housecat.
"Iceland is the new America." they said.

Have you ever seen all the heroic poems
and all the Icelandic Sagas?
It will take a sagacious mind and a month
to get through all of them!
I just look at any foreign languages
like you would at the surface of a painting.

Let's complain if we are alive.
Or write more poems at midnight.
We will run out of money and time
one fine day, and die in this cold.
We came to Iceland for some
internal revolution. Or inspiration?

We say: No, to the nothingness!

Book Three: Words and Things (1988)

A POEM FOR FRANK O'HARA

Are you familiar with the ancient song
"It was a stranger?" Pronounce it and then
let it rest. Now, there are no more troubadours
to sing fabliaux or love songs. But still
one can achieve a meaningless embrace
from some person who one does not know.

To him, there is what we call painting, and
he must explain why he is not a painter.
That's the trouble with a landscape and
with perspective: if perspective is only
an illusion, then why is the view so special?

It is difficult to be "historical," to have
time and space. Know yourself, in the sense
of the Bible as well, that is enough for a
lifetime. Medieval painters do not discount the
contributions of Rauschenberg and Pollock.

Walk through cardboard doors because long ago
there were men, and now there are men
made of cardboard and fragments.

BURYING THE ASHES

My memory has disappeared, and
maybe you were right about it all.
Why do you ask me?
Life used to be simple and meaningful,
and is no longer;
when I return to my room,
to hear the light wind:
this thought haunts me.
Leaves are swept away by someone.

At least there is heaven to hope for,
or is there? My doubt expressed jeopardizes
my chances of getting in now, at least
I can look at renditions by Italian painters.
When we leave, other life will evolve
for better or worse. I call you tonight
because I haven't a thought.

I heard the story not in its entirety,
the rain storm prevented me to travel
to another city. As I stare into the
gray mass, I envision a sunset that
I cannot see, orange and without form,
but precise as only words can be,
someone always prefers to spit instead of say.

RUTH

I have nothing to say to you
that will not upset you.
A dark brown color
inherits the earth.

In South America
the sun is taller, and the air
agrees with you.
Women from Mexico are superior, to use
a convenient superlative.
I'd rather not make comparisons if you
don't mind. I'll leave it at
that. The night fades in brown.

A woman gathers her dark powers.
Alcohol only enrages my mind;
dyed blond hair is acceptable
right now. Evening is upon us.
A scene of a whore in a shower
and you there covered with

water and her.
Even a long yellow light will find
some place to sleep.

LA PITTURA METAFISICA

Trouble begins when there is
a canvas within a canvas,
or when too many clouds appear
as if they are suspended rocks.

"This is not a cloud, but
a similitude, when the precision
and correctness of life shows
that something has gone awry."

Life here, as portrayed by the
lines of the architectural blueprints
and sketches, is life after the
disaster: where reason said to
itself "have you any reason left?"

Magritte knew it, as I drank my
coffee so that I would wake up from
this "life as a dream." Something
has gone awry. The explosion.

THE APPLES

To name is to make something
something else, to turn inward to
the imploded space, the blackness
which accepts those objects having
an appellation; the word which
infiltrates the object to the core.

When the object speaks
to me with secret noise
I feel that I must respond
by saying the word.

To make appeals to suspend
the death sentence: "to name
is to murder." The suspension
of time in the still-life, the
moment of time preserved, and
isolated; and the insides are
removed to save the skin.

It appalls. Those museums have
spider webs in the corners and
those paintings have died soon after
the painters have.

RAIN

No two rain drops are exactly alike,
and no shadows. Do we give a
rain drop respect when we name
it as if it no different from
a brother or a sister?

We name so that we pretend understanding,
but that does not prove anything
though it classifies and arranges
our experience in an order, but a
useful order, so that we may compare
the copies with the originals.
I can enjoy the silent world
without giving nominations.

To name we should name each object
we encounter; the sun today I will
call John. Like a silly book

report on some novel we were forced
to read, to compare and to contrast.
But "to contrast," that was the most
important thing; to distinguish
the drops from the flakes.

THE MIRROR OF JOURNALISM

This is not a portrait of God,
he knocks a double to the wall
and perfects his average. For this
time of year it is strange how
the clouds darken the sky in late
afternoon, and I do not understand.

I would like to walk through
a gallery, to read a book, and to just
live and to be able to appreciate
the newly born. It takes years of work,
of sacrifice, but to whose gain?

If all endure the writings, it is all
who'll benefit. But all neither can
endure nor can read the words.

It is not a matter of losing illusions,
or being bored.
"I have reported what I saw
and heard, for the rest of it:
I have no words."

EXILE

The earth built itself when we were not looking
with a preference for reptiles at first,
and when the moon drove across the sky, it approved.
A gap occurred and the sea rushed in from nowhere
while death claimed us with its heavy arms.
What was lifeless improvised a breath
and stayed for dinner.
He walked through the house
and laid down on the couch
and put his legs on the furniture.

He made advances, but to no avail.
She refused him, as she should, because
she had decided that he is no good.

Trees were arranged by construction workers
and he turned on the lamp called the sun.
The children were spoiled but that
will give him an excuse to kick them out
of the house when they are old enough.
Tell them to pack their bags.

They'll take apples, oranges, old sticks,
and some candy and put them in a suitcase,
and then they'll hope for rain
to prevent them from leaving right away.
The parents might change their minds
they'll think.

But fortunately it's summer, and it never rains.
Here is the brown earth waiting for the kill.
The roots are broken and are in shards.
Who needs them?

ROSES

Next to steel, we arrange a clever
scheme to give each other head, and
I showed my technique to you that was
rather rapid. Some people derive pleasure
from watching things die, or it would
seem so on the surface, and then
it is that they have sympathy in museums.
I remember white roses and red roses
lying all about the place, till they
become artifacts. The stiffness of dead roses.
Stones are slightly more inanimate than
the roses, but then the same,
even the discolored ones.

THE WIND

At last we meet in this chance encounter;
she puts flowers in glass vases as
I sit in the corner and drink coffee.

You used to say "so much to do and
so little time." Then it's ten years later
and you never moved a finger. Yet
the wind knows that nothing makes an
impression unless it comes with pain.

Your excuse was "his ambiguities have
left me in a desultory fever."

Those several letters which you did not
read, nor wanted to because they were
spiteful, landed somewhere with the
missing faces and all those names you
cannot remember. With glasses raised
high. Something about the end of each
year causes me to want to skip it.

The wind is always the wind, never knowing
itself, renewing itself. And then you
see how all your childhood friends
have become old and gray. It's not that
youth and innocence disappear with your
experience, on the contrary it is good
to be enthusiastic about life, but
that youth may have never been.

DOUBLE ANECDOTE IN CHINESE

There were two paintings
in the room.
Each of them told an old story.

A man who was drunk
disappeared and left his family behind.
His son went in a desperate search
for his father.
For ten years he found no trace of him.
Then one night the son gave up the search
and went to a bar to get drunk.
After sound and speech
became utterly undecipherable to him,
he tried to walk home.
He could barely stand upright
and on the way he collapsed
and slept beneath a tree.
That night he found his father.

In a village near the Yellow river
a man was caught in the act of cannibalism.
He was brought to the judge,
the wise man of the village.

All the people gathered around to hear
the punishment that the judge
would give to the cannibal.
They expected banishment or death.

The judge appeared, looked at the man,
and announced that there would be no
punishment given.
But he said to the man:
"you must remember that whatever you eat
in this life will eat you in your next life."

POETRY TAKES PLACE ON THE WINTER OF PAGES

It takes the place of things
such as rivers and mountains
and by that predilection or
recurrence votes for
the silent world.
When all was
flowing and unbridled
it was alive and artless
desiring some future day when
time would be still;
things frozen in the suspension of art.
And take pleasure in the living,
the palpable.
Later words were fragments
of the bough
on the white snow, the cold of the page.

If this life suddenly emerges as paradise,
let it be that and
do not foul it up.
And if a bird extends its wings
before you,
look at that view with intelligence.

SWIMMERS ON THE BEACH IN ITALY AND HERE

Only the moon is cold.
The lights on the water are
at once surface and reflection.
White circles moving
from side to side
in those paintings that Fred likes
much more than I do.
Those that we saw in Los Angeles.

Nude swimmers
and the several attempts
to capture the fickleness of water.
Above stars might be shifting
as you say, but it might be you.
I took a photograph.
But the visual does not
reveal the voice and the hidden.
When it's powerful,
that is the moment exceeding description.
The untold and the secretive allow
me to be what I am.
It is impossible to tell an old man
the news.
He has to unlearn the phases of the moon
and all that common knowledge.
When something new does not quite fit in
with something said already, there's an overflow.
How to understand the waves that are always
flowing and never standing still.
(I thought that we were neither).
You must run along to keep up
and not be kept with your pants down.

NIGHT SONG

Though times I am sad, this is no place to dwell upon it,
and once other things take place in my mind and arrive into
gear, arresting them as they accept the invitation,

sadness and pain are forgotten like water or leaves
on the sidewalk. How I struggled with biological terms:
once I understood them they seemed to be resting

in my mind with all the other words as if they were always
there, never learned. Now, it's a liquidity that goes in
and rarely goes out, and we make hidden and infrequent

what's going on inside: that is, a sexy dryness. But
change is what we are all about, and although we think
we do not change and that things do not change

because we recognize one day from another, those
familiar things and familiar airs of our different lives,
all things dissipate into something else

although we try to make out similarities
to comfort ourselves. That's the problem
I wanted to tell you tonight.

THE DEPARTURE OF THE POET

"I'll be leaving soon someday."
I used to tell myself when
by myself. In the afternoon
the shadows are long and speak
of some unknown structure or
facade which I cannot see.
I let a woman pass in
front of me.
We are leaving for Italy.

The arches of the building
are endless, I walked down
those halls which lead me
to a thousand places.
He takes my ticket. My
memory of statues and the people
are all one to me, but that
which remained unnameable, just
outside of my perception gave
me much more pleasure.
We are leaving for Italy.
My memory of dreams
is like my memory of the past.
The past is poetry, and
the future is nothing.
The train is departing.

CIGARETTES

You are as ephemeral as a puff
of smoke, lovers enter the dance
as the chorus or the refrain.

We met at the art gallery after
I had read your writings.

It started out as a solemn sketch,
then they multiplied, the position
of the body. Sometimes there is no
threat to discredit from other people,
and if it hurts, it is partly your
own doing. Unobstructed and clear,
the view of the room. Those were
the few years when we all lived
together in the same part of the city.
You could never leave me.

Our days disappeared like abandoned
or forgotten lovers, then everything
was old. Prices rose, and we all
tried to gamble. Friends passed
as white as ghosts. A portrait will not
age like a woman, but it may die.

THE SKIN

Now that I have you, your attention
not disappearing and it follows the edges.
Another abandoned building was destroyed
to make room for the new, but all
cities need some old buildings to
reminds us, to show us clearly how
"new" is the new. Bricks are now
for fences, not skyscrapers.
What is important is that which
remains constant throughout time.
You can only ignore what you
have known very well.

We could remain
youthful in our minds, but we do not.
Time and experience is
written on the skin: the world outside
pressing its mark, and your world in
your mind. And whatever you can believe,
what the mind is capable of belief, that
should stay. A layer that embodies
each history, the journey of one.
It's what holds the insides in.

The fragments, a stone column with
marble, bones, and old books.
A painting is also a sort of skin which
begins as a blank slate, then is filled
with being and knowledge, then sheds its
skin when reality becomes too much
of a heavy burden to wear.

THE BEES

The prairie is the beginning (the
before) of it all, as a bee flies
in the imagination or in a field.
Jupiter agrees with Mars, I
drink the water. To be is the
act of being: one must take
the stings with the stains.
Allow me to be brief, the spirit
of the pratum (meadow) reveals itself
after long study. I am prepared
to be accountable for the re-establishment
of the past, as should be everyone.

Our parallel histories are recreation
though contained within a strict form
of notation, the earthworks in motion
while the memory (the eye) as a sponge.
Trees multiply, they engender themselves
in complete indifference. The massive
elevation of mountains. The bee lives
in the midst of this. nearby a gathering
of people singing in the key of b.

I DRAW A BLANK

What does one do when sitting
in a car but to remember all those
novels that one will never read?
To read about "the cold winter"
in summer, a feverish heat,
will make one turn on the furnace
or rather it will cool one off
as if it was a drink one had.
But to read about us, those
who she will never know, will take
careful concentration and quiet,
and decision about all those endless
pages of prose. Then you ask:
"how can she make up her mind
about us so early on in her
reading, why close the book when not
going on to the second chapter and
eventually finishing?" Either those pages
are blank, haven't been lived yet,
or as she said in her frank
way: "you are boring reading."

THE ORANGES

The landscape painter paints
Some geometrical shapes and shadows.
I talked him into it, of course.
He paints with his eyes close,
Rejecting experience in favor of
His internal world, if he has one.
The painter asks me "What did you
Have for breakfast this morning?"
I laugh out loud.
"Just make it up, there's nothing
in us, and there's nothing in it.
But we have an excuse. We can
Pretend that the world exists,
If it is already established. See?
It works. But that is not art!"
He paints a still-life, a tableau,
With oranges. Beautiful soup.

SONG OF THE BUSHES

Bushes, an object of scorn,
Well overlooked in great novels
And even sentimental poetry.
The parks of the world, rows
Of neglected shrubbery, weeds,
Sticks, garbage, and brown bushes.
A painter with his every mistake,
The addition of bushes in between
The rough edges of mountains
And rivers. Wilderness. The solitude
Of the dark forest. No attention
Given, by its own request.
And Shakespeare: "Good wine
Needs no bush."
That is, by advertising its
Quality and hiding its flaw.
The trompe de l'oeil, the
Curtain parts, to speak of
Other things.

SEMEN

The bull rushes out
the door,
he is recalcitrant and moves
around the arena.

The dark hemisphere
and the light one.
We are indifferent to the sun,
as far as our purposes go, it is black.
Magnanimous people can watch wars as
well as sports: pull
the string and the kite
will move towards the lightning.
Here is the foundation of the church.

Is there ever any true reparation
when something is forgiven?
Here's the seed,
somewhere in this
is the pith of the thing
which will make it grow
but it does not have to.
It may decide to be barren and
there is nothing that can be done.

Opening the door to
the sun
when the outside becomes the inside
and we cannot
tell the difference.

MINDS THAT EXPLODE IN SLEEP

Some nights are a sentinel with too many worries.
Was that color brown or sepia and did
Did I experience it or was I told about it?
I should be sent to the desert or some secluded city.
Some people prefer to sleep.
They enjoy it and they do it well.
All for different reasons: some have
good dreams, and some are sleepwalkers
and eat during the night.
Others enjoy the danger of nightmares.
Some leave on the radio.
Some have sex with the television on and
they leave it on all night with little notice.

I liked the orchard behind our house
because one could run around there and play,
eat oranges, and take a nap very easily.
There was a German novelist who told me he had
flawless memory.
It was just how he was.
And when he went to bed he would just knock off
right away into the twilight world.
He could fall asleep whilst sitting in a chair.
I do not know why it's me who cannot sleep,
and what is it that keeps me awake?
The thought that others are sleeping soundly?
I should be thrown in the sea.
The room is cold.
I am alone in my bed at home.

PLEASURE

Even after eternity and us
there will be things like ice cream and gin and tonic.
If you believe in pleasure, sex, music,
movies, and more, then convert me over
to the new religion.
It becomes a habit too fashionable
to be complaining all the time,
and does it matter and is it to any avail?
So let the problems sink into
the background for the moment, and let
friends and alcohol replace them.
I enjoy the intensity of the moment,
but that is not all.
And sure life is a celebration as well as a discipline.
Every moment should be equal, and
there is no tomorrow.
A man wants to be admired for an achievement,
but why him more than another?
Someone who has time for you rather than the world?
It is not you or myself or him or her that I love
because each moment the self blends
into the opposite.
She wants to follow the several faces
of herself and her desires over the years,
not one of them is she.

THE ISLAND OF THE DEAD

Our world is largely ignored,
the trees of the imagination,
no island river, the rocks and mountains
metamorphose into cities and buildings.

Remember Italy?

Those many summers we spent
in Rapallo and at art school;
we do not belong here.

Our visits in the imagination.
We come here to forget,
this is our heaven.
As reality withdraws from us and becomes
"something that we missed out on" we
withdraw from the ghost that remains.
That is the thing I cannot tell to another person.

By boat we travel here, and I pray:
I sign my motto on the marble stone.
"There's no guide for us,
we must dream our own dreams,
to create again, by our own light."

Book Four: Genghis Khan's Daughter (1989)

JUST ME

Yes I am like that,
torn like a half-page note
with a recipe scribbled on it,
blue like a watercolor.
I know those words and those tedious notes
and I remember them when
on the back of the Fillmore bus.
I'm not sure who I am
or what I amount to
because I haven't finished,
yet I am always beginning
and ending, ending without closure.

And like music there is a time, and a place.
There are rests, and profound moments.
One can fall into speech so easily,
with beautiful tones that suggest imagined pictures
of places with names like Mazatlan.

Most arrangements are like this:
me, words, and sounds.
How many symphonies or
cathedrals are left unfinished!
The pen is in my hand,
I am lying on my bed,
it is evening,
the letter is not done,
I have drank and have ate some food,
and the weather has been good.

FEUERBACH

You will go into the future
without residue or notes.
You will climb inside my skull
and my emptiness will nourish you.
Feuerbach doesn't agonize over one word.

The notes of distant music enters
your mind, and will want to go there
one day. Life is a difficult climb
and you left your notes behind.

You had brilliant eyes and thoughtful
moments during sunsets.
You were once so full of death
and worms.

You had been bitten by fleas
and other insects as you prayed.
You prayed to the silence,
and now you have this song.

INTELLECTUAL VIETNAM

November: Yes, get out the white snuffbox.
Dear me, I must respond to your note and briefly erase
the misconceptions about the palatable and the digestible
spirit in you, and the means to simplify yourself.

Beyond that is someone's pleasure barking.
Smoke fills the black room: there's talk.
An audience coughs when I write my story.
I have never heard of the other "you."

A catharsis? Fuck you, you got to be kidding.
I am really indifferent towards.... "the personal bores me"
says the ghost of Jack Spicer. Art is not an apolitical attack
on reality, but a bed of nails to sit on.

So, you have an interest in "urban writers?"
I have rated the writers you have mentioned.

Old goat: who continues to be name-dropped.
Not of any use, but shows that you're well-read.

Cream-puff: a martyr who is praised
by the young, and who will soon be forgotten.

Computer nerd on speed: who writes and writes
and who has never heard of living.

Blanchot without the juice: middle aged American
who obviously has a French connection.

And a lot of hot air if you can't breathe anymore.

Angst? Depression? What a cop out!

Ass end of metaphysics? Itself is the reality.
I am amazingly bored with you, the poem.
I am also bored with my face in a mirror.
Patience is good, but boredom is bad for me.

This is my one chance at life and I am learning.
I am patient enough to find a good hat for life.
Let me explain: all the best hats are profound,
while some poems have no hat at all.

Have you seen the pictures of our youth?
It's cute and meaningless being that young.
The singer is still on the stage waiting....
Is it time? To wring his neck? Poor Laszlo!

In every room go solo, snakebitten
the untried wishes, maybe this is life standing
in the hallway with some sort of uniform
walking on carpets that offer trust
refuse to lose rhetoric and trouble
I've got so much trouble, pooh
black king attack, paranoid, pooh-pooh
expose the flesh, terror in your ears
raw metaphysical errors and apologies
I'm the hustler of culture
dropping the bomb
the color, uncover
undercover and quiver

But about my bus business
with trying to write a poem.
I will write more. Please no more!
A novel this year? Maybe not.

BLACKBURN SONGS

The dead never dream
of the living
or anything in their past.
Only white remains.
White.

White.

White.
20 degrees Fahrenheit.
46 degrees north.
93 degrees west.

Down the freeway
I went nowhere, nowhere.
I went to where the dead
never dream.

White fences, white sidewalks.
"These houses are very old" you said.
But when where they built?
How old are they?

I wished that I could have met Blackburn
in the dead man's dream.
I could have embraced him,
and told him that I understood.

No one listens to anyone else
most of the time.
They tell me to go to New York City,
or London, England, and they will listen to me there.

Great works must be written still,
by anyone, at any cost.
The real poet takes the oilcloth
and wipes the canvas clean.

Now I am no longer interested
in dead people.
I could care less about dead places and dead things.

I care only about the oilcloth.

By emptying their songs.

BROTHERHOOD OF THE GRAPE
(for David Harding)

Silence until this: which our frozen youth
is in cold isolation. Listen to three that were
one. The brotherhood was everything to me
and I turned my back on it.

I stand before a blank wall, and a dead end.
Having sung every song of truth that is known.
Trusting language to be real skin (sentence of life).
Turning to black from our last friend on earth.

I managed to define the "self" as a mobile, fluid self.
Now they call me "thief" and they call me "liar."
I must now look like some abandoned animal.
The void inside me remembers being on a wrecked ship.

More beastly I have become with the days passing.
Having lost my way and my good friends.
While the drifting me, the landless, does not owe you
or this world, or time itself, or anything real.

By choosing such treachery and selfishness to survive,
I have lost you forever with deep regrets.
I have lost my youth, and maybe the future too.
My ruined self still breathes today, the wreckage continues.

THE WORLD IS BLUE

Parallel instances of swallowed dreams.
Unheard are the frustrations of logic.
Are you ready to go for a ride?
I have no idea where. Yes, look it up.

Overpowered by the stronger army.
Blood is a good lubricant.
Changing as we do, but dead men never change.
I seek the eruption, the sun rises with gold.

The moon itself in the false clouds.
She's the one who made this miserable world.
My old champion was tarred and feathered.
Join the circus, and pink skin will shed.

Loosen the load as blood's season fades.
On desolate sand and in solitude.
Let's wake up the red girl today.
Bodies ripped open by excess....

Portraits of the family: father's didactic speech.
Hearing with two ears, or listening with
two voices. You have no choice.
I say again: "You have no choice."

GENGHIS KHAN

Unfit for spring because
the year called too early.
An urgent message:
Left many sentences undone.

First, an aggressive radiance.
And the rest added up to much less
than what was previously expected.
Paradise is everywhere but here on earth.

I need a small room of my own
for slight improvements.
A slight surplus of pine trees
was the latest gossip.

Science classes and German armies
confirmed this to me.
Acquisition of land was desired
by the straw boss.

Armies marched into the Ukraine.
As I watched this, I was reminded
of my sexual orientation. Zinc and mountains
were somehow involved in the decision.

Genghis Khan's daughter
has a hot ass.
Suffering and tyranny gave way
to a new vibrant culture.

It was as if a rigorous new order
allowed the mind certain liberties.
Yes. The Mongols have paved the way
for poets like Paul Blackburn.

It's all a golden age
full of air and pomp.
We all make mistakes:

some are forgotten, some on the world's stage.

I get carried away sometimes.
I shoot large cannonballs
at the night armies
and trains that cry "Peace!"

Months later the empire is quartered
and given out to lesser talents.
A few con artists with
diplomas in the liberal arts.

We are the company that gave
you zinc and mountains.
The only place for the pure artistic mind
is in isolation.

I have a headache because
the daily routine is just devastating.
The music outside my window
is cold and violent.

MARTINIQUE

Including everything, the lines which stretch out to the boundaries; then we desire nothing. This maybe be conclusive evidence for desire, or severely scratching wild claims of love, or the impossible. At least we agree that it appears impossible. Yet today, we do not know the boundaries entirely, even though yesterday we thought we did. Of yesterday, all I remember is that we fucked each other, so it resembled many other days. We grew up in a certain environment, and the relations remained unchanged. The only answer to immobility is to diffuse and to differ, to spread out the development of our lives, this ongoing fiction, over entire days. What is it to live in the space of entire days, and not just parts? What is it that I identify with are the sentences and the voices of the recent past. The pauses included. This space where I am infinitely free. To disclose and to conceal. I am only free in these words which arrange themselves on a page and somehow appear true to themselves.

Then forms appear. Things take on a significance, and I become less important. But that is just the background becoming the foreground. The details add up. I do not live in a vacuum, surely. In writing and also in reality. What appears vague at first, then more defined. The shore. The waves crash on the shore. The moon behind the clouds. These are just parts of the whole. Descriptions. Details. There is more to find somewhere. More. It is desire that makes me find the other. What other? The outside. Silence.

OTTER JITTERS

Placing a corsage on the unguent dress
of a prom date I never knew, in a Midwestern state.
Knocking on doors, I have a divine fever like a
cursive gunshot of heroin. Nerves tell me to jot
this note, yet I may be the next brutalized corpse
to litter the smoky battlefield. Bodies wrapped like gifts.
The sadistic knife cuts the eye, affliction unknown.
The straitjacketed senses are bracketed from memory.
Fulmination gases the patients before the operation.

In reverie, I am the anti-hero in doctor's drag.
Is it distraught milk of the postman's wife
or those vagina walls dripping butter that
nourish me during a breakfast in the antipodes?
Or is love anathema to a higher spiritual hex?
Our last troubled conversation, nothing but the torn
metal of thin skin, coffee adorned with whipped
cream, emollients, and dog collars.

Like that pink corsage dripping the seas
on a lapel for hours, your imprecation holds
my attention while the unmemorable band strikes
up some old forgotten song of the seventies.

Like some bone babies hiding
in torpid wombs for ages,
the sea holds the helix of a gun
with its unreal rats asking me for
the real reason I wrote this?

Between us is the silent infinity of dead
space that cannot be traversed
but still our bodies try to close the sex, the gap.
Scarred skin exudes a lucky excrement.
Her salesman framed the impact and the pace
jotting the infected rogue with maximum defect.

I see her in a dress. Who?
Breasts like carnage under a shoelace.
Dead letters never returned. All the tortured
things to do with incompetence
and fragmented speech of hospitals.
All that you wish to complain about.
His saliva was like urine wishing
for a crystal dream with potent smell.
Can you imagine these words coming
forth, rolling from your own lips?
Repeat slowly after me.

You can speak back but do not,
and prefer to drool during a recess.
I perfectly understand the will to stand over.
I see her in a dress the others thought was hideous.
She was the wound that the world
caused by self-afflicted torture.
I am not a hero or a shoulder
to drive on, to take a nap.
I live dutifully in carnage prison.
As beautiful as a tall white Rasta
a clean can of spaghetti, circus
tents and driveways of princes.

SHE'LL CALL IN THE DOGS

A.L.M. –

Sorry, it began. Then the blue woman stepped out of the black car with her poodles, thought of us as detectives, and warned us about the imminent future. "Look to the East. Find my Genghis, my dear Genghis. Genghis is good for you!" she said.

I drank the dregs of my warn beer, and actually we all tilted our glasses up high in unison, and then I dramatically recalled the words of an older poet, or who knows who said it? I didn't. The blue woman started to mumble. She started to speak in tongues. She dreams of unstable forms which she described to me in detail: Long lines of people wandering through fields trying to find something important, or better yet, trying to achieve something damnable so that forgiveness comes quick. Next, by all the rocks, the water falls over itself in this manner (she gestured with her hand), and it doesn't matter. Yet when the last bird-wings are divided among the poor to eat, the birds suffer because they are not symbolic. We all do suffer not knowing which way is up, not knowing bread from stone, or which is the way home. There are no buses in this neighborhood past ten o'clock. Do not ask a woman for directions. They will send you off into the dark. You tried to sniff out their resources and they tied up the communications. You find out later that the edge of the forest is where the lost meets itself.

Do not wake the gods for they are sleeping, and have been for centuries, or are just dead with paint brushes in their hands. They know the humiliation of the failed artist, and they know how to fail. They could not paint anything other than themselves, and soon one gets tired of such self-reduction plans. When they were poor and gave away every portrait, every brushstroke, and every hour of work. There was nothing left and they all stood there naked. You can look back and mourn. The mythic mind has left us, history has disappeared, and the poet of today stands alone with empty hands.

Whatever the blue woman actually said was forgotten, and not written down. I do remember her last few statements. She said: "Women will rise in the world." She said: "The best thing about the 1970s was 1890." She said: "Give in to the system. The system will always be here and will outlive you. It's you who are extinct and will die and perish. I will not let you fuck me anymore. I am the system."

A FEW HAIKUS

A few days, summer is over, sadly.

Your letter came, it pleased me, silence.

Drank wine, violet sky with wind, the cats are fixed.

The tape of Mendelssohn, the door closes, the second moon.

He changes his mind, a restaurant, the journey home.

Flowers, the birth of a butterfly, our shared prayers.

I made my visit, clouds, noises.

The sea, the thought of Italy, room of my old friends.

A meeting, the bee keeper, the view at the airport.

The telephone rings, long walks, later I read then slept.

Ice water, sleep without dreams, pleasant calm hours.

Movement, according to what, those feelings.

No money, no lovers, no worries.

I read all day, words like insects, pages like wings.

A beautiful face, the another, the garden unfolds.

Disappearing, disappearance, yesterday and moments.

Matisse remembered timelessness, beautiful moment, only I swam.

Sun, moon, the intelligence of man.

BASEBALL PREDICTIONS FOR THE 1989 SEASON

AMERICAN LEAGUE

EAST
1. New York
2. Toronto
3. Boston
4. Detroit
5. Milwaukee
6. Cleveland
7. Baltimore

WEST
1. Oakland
2. Texas
3. Kansas City
4. Minnesota
5. Seattle
6. Chicago
7. California

NATIONAL LEAGUE

EAST
1. New York
2. Montreal
3. Pittsburgh
4. St. Louis
5. Philadelphia
6. Chicago

WEST
1. San Francisco
2. Cincinnati
3. Houston
4. Atlanta
5. Los Angeles
6. San Diego

THE UNDERSTUDY

The actor in the wings,
in the curtains he hides studying
the words on a page; someone else
is sharpening knives. The music
comes from the orchestra pit.
The play is a story about an archaeologist
named Remi Chelveucaux who travels
to Central Africa in the year of 1830.
He lives with a tribe for six years:
he learns the dialect of the tribe,
he lives as one of the tribe.
Their language has no verbs and no nouns.
When Chelveucaux returns to France to reveal
his research, he dies from a rare disease,
and his research becomes undecipherable.
On the fifth night of the play the lead actor
becomes sick, which turns out to be
a similar disease to the one in the play.
The understudy takes the place of the sick man
in the role of Chelveucaux.
He weighs less than the sick man,
so the clothes must be altered.
His costume is restored,
his talents with needle and thread.

TWO CITIES

1.

Ah, Francesco, where is the book?
The stores were closed today,
and all of San Francisco was closed today.
I had stuffed potatoes
and they filled me up.
I burnt the rice earlier
because I was on the telephone too long.
I'm always on the telephone.

2.

Every day when
I wake up
I want to meet
a new person,
someone
new, who I can
love.
Someone
who I
can spend at least
a day in
bed with.

3.

Is there a new
place to go to?
I don't know of it.
I want to be carried away.
With someone or something.
Where can I
go where
I can meet
you,
who are beautiful?

4.

No friends
that will help out.
Do they care?
What do they care about?
Yesterday I found
a book of poetry
that I had been
looking for,
for a few weeks.

5.

My father lived
and died on these
streets.
His blood is
still on
Leavenworth street.
Only I see it.

6.

No one remembers
my father on
these streets.
No poets.
No one remembers
the dead
in this town.
Everyone without
a past.

7.

I have to
remember to get
my shoes tomorrow.
Sometimes I
write about nonsense
and draw pictures.
We're not
on the freeway yet.

8.

The legal process
tells me who's who
in the future
or where to find
Audrey Hepburn
in a magazine.
Two women pass
by with umbrellas.
It's still raining
in New York City.
Why all this attention
to the weather?
Because it's to figure out
how to dress.
It was 70 degrees
yesterday, in February!

9.

What are the great ideas
of our time?
My back hurts.
I need to have
a massage every day.
Heavy metal is on the way out.
Good ideas are always
good ideas.

I read a collection of
comics by Doug Allen
called "Steven."
West Broadway?

10.

I read the novel
called
"the novel."
It wasn't easy
to read.
It's about a boy
named George Stable.
He lives on
West 3rd street
and Sixth avenue.

11.

Stan Gontarski
can't make it to NYC.
He just finished
a translation
to be published
by Barney Rosset.
I talked to Barney
about a job.
He said "can't help you,
times are tough."
Planes are
expensive
over Brooklyn skies.

12.

Employed
by welfare.
The children
with their teenage
mothers.
A sister.
The moon
in a wheelchair,
pasted to the
walls
advertisements.

13.

Woody Allen is
a guy from Brooklyn.
I'm not.
I'm from far away,
a place called
San Francisco.
No one here
recognizes the existence
of that beyond the Hudson.
No one leaves Manhattan.

AFTER THE KANGAROO

1.

As soon as the idea of the kangaroo had subsided, a penis stopped among the feathers and the swaying vagina, and said his words to the kangaroo through the feathers.

Oh, the precious vaginas that began to hide! The penises already looking about them! In the kangaroo, words were set up, and the feathers were hauled down to the vagina which rose in penises, as in old kangaroos.

Penises flowed: at vaginas in the kangaroos, in the words, where a feather's seal turned the penises pale. Vaginas flowed, and words.

Kangaroos built. Vaginas steamed in the little feathers.

In the big penis, which was still dripping, the kangaroos in mourning looked at the marvelous vaginas.

A word banged, and on the feathers the kangaroo waves his penis, and was understood by vaginas and penises on kangaroos everywhere under the bursting feather. Madame kangaroo installed a penis in the vagina. Words and first feathers were celebrated at the hundred thousandth kangaroo. Penis set out. And the kangaroo was built in the words of vagina and penis.

(Arthur Rimbaud)

2.

Pasolini: oral stimulation of the penis. I am looking at your face, you cross your legs. We are spectators of each other. We adopt a cool, neutral tone. We sit in a room, and although there are many people here, I am aware of only two. So are you. As soon as my mind was made up, I tried to rape the sky and the clouds. My cock banged against your

pussy, loudly, and the violence shouted my name "devil."
Hell-ward I was going. Shit, I was proud and I didn't care. I
poured gasoline down your throat. The throat of the pussy
which choked on the violence of my name. My name? I have
lived and I am not regretting it. More and more.

Minette: to engage in sexual intercourse. Open your lips.
Saying something is better than your silence. I once took a
needle and thread and sewed up your cunt, but that was long
ago. Can you forgive me? Can hate last forever? Let try to
make it last. Your face hid beneath a mask and I am looking
for you behind my mask. I have been searching for years and
haven't found you. What will be our scenario? How will it
play? It's all a game. It's real simple. Do you want to play?
You can go hide. I am hiding, too.

Anne: to seize especially with the teeth or jaws so as to enter,
grip, or wound. I laugh in your face, you pathetic old hag.
You junkie! I refuse! I am silent. I am the silent one. I am
Rimbaud, not you. The river that flows out of the pussies is
where I drink, mixed with hot come. My sperm mixed with
all lover's sperm. Kiss me, and taste it. It is evil. I could be
full of words, feathers enough to fill several pussies. The
cock is so hard and red and it wants to penetrate you. The
only thing that connects us is this cock. Whisper words in
the bed of feathers. Make no promises, never! No more
stories. Tell no more tales.

Sarah: to strike especially on the buttocks with the open
hand. I want to kill you, beat you, strangle you.... You are
too young. After me, you will know better. Your sister is here
in my arms and you cannot stand it! I built the house where
we will live and love and torture each other for four months.
I will not clean it. It will be time to leave. We will find other
lovers, we will always have time for other loves. This letter is
not an apology, although you may be wondering why you
haven't heard from me lately. I don't care. I am underground.
I am an asshole. I am perfecting the philosophy of
"Assholism." I did rip off seven hundred dollars from you,
and I have no feelings toward it. I am neutral. I have partied

with this money, drank alcohol and took too many drugs with it. And I made you believe that I wanted to buy a car! Ha! You fool! I am hiding in Vancouver. Good luck finding me.

Ariel: the act or practice of employing something. You are gone to Seattle. You left without my knowledge, but I let you go. I scared you. I was the cause of your worst nights. You remember that hell? Jump the difficulty of borscht, quiz the editor, you the vile zebra. Fix the memories which glide. A bobcat yawns. A whisper comes from Monsieur X's mouth and lands on the yolk of existence. Volkswagen on fire: look out! No crisis when you follow the Q. The jig dances a foul, a population of Kiev's ex-convicts. Patrick Quinn walks invisible through the room. Strong wind, being a zephyr, doesn't affect me. Cooling dirty water. The lines are busy, set a fire. It's a kiss. Juliette gives me head. The final dawn of quick instant borscht. X number of plums. Three? "Yes" the zebra was right.

Shea: to touch with the lips. I remember my childhood, and when I write your name I kill it. I do not know where to go. There are other men in this scenario. Other beautiful men. These films are not to be seen by anyone. Pasolini did not live to see it. You are without roots. We sit in a black room and read Fuck Journal and act it out.

Veronica: to offer indiscriminately for sexual intercourse for money. You should become a nun. You told me that you were going to use that money for rent. You probably went and smoked some crack with it. I met her on the street at three in the morning. She returned with me to my apartment. She was not expensive. I had some money. We smoked some hash.

Ruth: a woman who practices promiscuous sexual intercourse for hire. You're a whore! You are the devil. You are real. I see you and you see me. The room is full of mirrors and we look at each other from every side. I meet Ruth. Ruth fucks me. Boy and girl happy. Ruth leaves me. I kill Ruth. End. I kill, you kill, we kill, we kill, you kill, they kill, he kills, she kills.

Paris: abnormally averse to sexual intercourse. I just want to sleep, but I can't sleep. I stay up all night, and think about all the possibilities. What I should have said. What did I say. What I will say in the future. All scenes are real. Memories as real now as they were then. I think about philosophy, whatever. All of the thoughts that are possible. Given the circumstances. A light glows on every subject I can think of. I describe the situations and the objects. Then I think of the why of it all. Why it works. Soon, interest ceases.

Me and all the others, others who I've forgotten their names, enact the scenarios.

USE

Use this when all are asleep everyone blond hair the night
then the frost you love the rain perfume and think of when
you think it proper the cat tissue food and mirrors do not
forget about those nights last year the heater the rent at least
we were warm oatmeal hair dye television novels all those
blankets I like easier reading the heater the little one a
shadow in the darkness we used to sleep in a line our legs
together my stomach against your back my lips against your
neck sometimes my arm over your shoulder arms legs fingers
moving down there you said no no no not that this is hard to
read we never did it we did it constantly yet you meant not
now wait at least until the morning I am tired and we never
had any food had to go to that art gallery despised the
paintings ate crackers and wine that night till full of it you
made me drink more than I am comfortable drinking drunk
drunk I am a drinker not a lover why do you want to get me
drunk no money cash bucks then the fight I do not
remember who hit who first I did not get hit someone pored
some liquid in my face all over my jacket now later I read this
book in San Francisco years and faces and miles away that
jacket got it in the neck your cat pissed all over it dry cleaned
it ten times still smells we took a bath together later that
night but we recalled the fight in letter smack thump thud
bow bow bow thud drink slosh spilled mierda hey hey bow I
am going to kill you man hold him back hold back español
take this warm drink again the letter in my face thank you
very much for blindness mother I cannot see alcohol in my
eyes they are burning I did not get punched I did the punch
punching bow bow bow bah bah no no no not that one two
we never did it we did it shit constantly yet you meant not
now wait bob sisisbob at least until the morning tasting your
titties I am tired and we never had any food no no no but I
ate yogurt in the morning moor room always was it Sinclaire
or Sinclair eyesore eros eye the merder clarity of sin clear
sun the clearing of sin

ARRANGEMENT IN GREY AND BLACK

As time passes you become someone;
a man steps on a bus,
the trees become truly amazing,
a radio plays, the clouds overhead unnoticed,
the shadows rearrange themselves,
the postman arrives,
you drink lemonade,
the lamp is turned on,
the wind increases,
someone buys a hot dog,
a girl goes to school,
others ask me for spare change,
and the whole is still never the whole,
and thoughtfulness helps no one:
the painter mixes colors,
and our portrait is denounced as
"the work of students."

As events become less integrated
as when he said "I did not
know that she would step
in front of my car,"
still, events have a relationship
and a resonance though I
cannot explain it;
possibly you know this too, you demigod.

But surely I cannot
say something to you as simply
as I could have at one time
many years ago.
You give me panorama
and that does not explain anything.

BE CRUEL

baby you can drive my car
you can drive my car baby
can drive my car baby you
drive my car baby you can
my car baby you can drive
car baby you can drive my

I see myself as the shadow
see myself as the shadow I
myself as the shadow I see
as the shadow I see myself
the shadow I see myself as
shadow I see myself as the

it's all around us circling us
all around us circling us it's
around us circling us it's all
us circling us it's all around
circling us it's all around us
us it's all around us circling

the fields of your pink lives
fields of your pink lives the
of your pink lives the fields
your pink lives the fields of
pink lives the fields of your
lives the fields of your pink

TAURUS EARTH

My grandfather waited until my birthday to die. How kind of him! Now I will always remember him and think of him. All those tales. His blue teeth. His addiction to kool-aid. He told me a lot of stories. I never believe any except those proven by science.

A year later, my stepfather's father died close to my birthday too on April 26, the same day as the birthday as Ludwig Wittgenstein. His name was Emmanuel Schwartz and he was 89 years old. I met him twice. He looked like Spencer Tracy. He lived in old New York City. He worked on Canal street at the city prison. He worked there for many years, lived in the Bronx, and then retired to Fort Lauderdale, Florida.

I last saw him in 1978 when I went with my parents to his 50th wedding anniversary. I have a picture of myself in Miami, in a little suit and tie, wearing a Yarmulke.

This night was painted red. Painted by me. The voice was red. The floor was built and now roll out the carpet. We, as strangers, exchanged our painted voices. I cannot visit anywhere in this damn country without bringing superstitions. Who cares? Who cares what happens, what happens to England? We are living the last days of its empire. The fires are burning out. Stalingrad is as common knowledge as Ty Cobb's lifetime batting average. If you sleep with the cook, the soup will not taste any better. I don't care what Pamela Des Barres says.

Someone else dies after my birthday this year that I know. As we get older, we will have to deal with the death of family and friends. My high school reunion is this year, and I wonder how many of those people have died in the past ten years?

You look more and more like Mom. Surprise! In my pubic hair, monks are playing soccer. Read the letter held up to the sun. Any extras? The 18th century is mainly known for its wife-beaters. Step into that room with Blake, and drink its beer. A greasy taste of history with its lack of love.

You sleep and have nothing in common with your more enlightened contemporaries. Your neck through a noose, a cowboy like any American, and then hung to dry. An American burial. "Look, Mister Bo dangles."

May: our month of funerals. I suppose that my grandmother who is dear to me will die in May, and so will my brother. I will experience the impossible pain of their loss, their disappearance.

WHEN THE HENS GREW TEETH

Betty threw me the seeds
her ended fete wedded her green eyes
the seventh week the mensch, Mel, lets
beer settle the preferred bed-sheets
bells meet the length, legs defy sex
the pere, Lester, gets the eel
her frere, Teddy, the new egg
better yet streets end feckless testes
mere Zen never rests here
Mel, the newest pet bejeweled
pen prefers the net bent desert
let the red hex enter the tent
ten jeeps deem the news reel empty
kept green cement twelve weeks
wheel's rent peel the eyes
seeds next?
send them Rex, the sex mensch
the letters meet levers
greet them
feed them, Betty
me, the creep's fever

WHERE THE BODY GOES

1.

I start anew, the triple exposure, blurred photography where
clapping means little, and polite laughter is a balloon that
pops. I can imagine my face in the other person's mind, but
what face is it? I do not understand you. We hurt each other
often, sometimes with fiction. Sometimes with bricks. How
do you understand those distant places? They battle, but it's
not our battle. We only understand winner and losers. I wake
up, turn on the radio, wait. I turn on the hot water, and wait.
Only this time the pain is real. It is difficult. I do not know
how two people can arrange a meeting. Accidental
arrangement. This conversation includes everybody, so join
in when you want to. Someone I know is boarding a plane to
Amsterdam.

2.

Finally felt good when
I woke up this morning,
which has been rare recently. And then,
after having read much Firbank: it did not take
my mind off the current matters.
All my problems.
It's this area in San Francisco
where I live now.
It's so separate, isolated.
It's also quiet.
It takes a while to get anywhere else.
No place that I would want
to go is close by.

I've lost weight.
New clothes.
I feel that my body is different.

3.

Merry ha ha. One day in time is worth a hundred in death. The laundromat attendant leaves me to join the demonstration. "I thought you were never coming back" she said. Laughter becoming sadness, sad laughter, in a long drawn out scene in some improvised movie my Dad wouldn't have let me see when I was thirteen. Now, I am thirteen plus thirteen plus one day in time. So alone that it makes you want to cook a meal for two.

You spend only so much time on this earth, and so much more time in the cold ground. Why waste it waiting in line, or working for a cause that you could care less about? Do what gives you pleasure.

4.

"I'm trying to write something for you, for your birthday...." the letter began. I take a deep breath. It's time to sleep alone and desire you who are not here.

5.

There is a party attended mostly by women. I am there too. At L's house. It is L's birthday party possibly. We all drink and talk. It gets late and a younger girl, S, begs L to stay over. S wants to sleep over for some unknown reason. She is attracted to L, I would guess. L tells S to go into her bedroom. L tells me that she is going to fuck around with this younger girl, S. L is not attracted to S. L wants to play games with her mind. They go to bed together.

6.

Her body is the most powerful being I know. I identify with her. I want to be her. I don't know who the fuck she is. I would like to kill her and take her place. I would like to be that young girl who she takes into her room and fucks, and fucks with her mind. I would like her to destroy me. I would like to know why. But maybe if I knew "why" her body wouldn't be so fascinating. Maybe I should remain on the outside.

Her body shouldn't be the most powerful being that I know. I should be. I should be my only hero. Her body will have to go. I do not understand her body. She does not understand my body. I will not see her anymore. I will not let her control me. I will ridicule her whole life. She is the center of nothing. I am the center. I say this out of love for the body.

I am not the center.

7.

The black and gold bottle shaped into an owl said "Made in Lyon." The note inside is forged. All about friendship that I question now. I had a brief conversation with the gay eel, and it reported the facts about how to suck a breast. Once a daughter. And you know how the body can change shapes: can you follow the transformations? Boy, was that a steep symphony that I just dove into. I stuck out my hand out of the water and a dream ends. Say "hey" when you touch bodies beneath the waist. Look up, and look out for water. I learned that dance from those weird Incas. The fat is gone. Center-less. You have to be in touch with your roots. Watch out, this body will tear easy.

8.

The force that through the purple penis drives the yellow diction, scimitar by Mr Henry Brenlar, the choice of abandonment or hope. Or, if you like, I may become a Vikings fan for the practice of pitting the vile zebra against the alphabet. Bad call. Shit scrape off his shoes, the twilight was broken by the repetition of a revolver ricocheting off the marble in a palace in Marienbad; a woman who was too violent (a violent temper that has always plagued women), ensued violence trapped within tits and lips and pussy prepared to pit any plum.

9.

Eyes which look on me like they do
the intricacies of a little motor,
yet the blimp was not invented
with my birth.
       Perhaps the words
"user friendly" were? I look
at you and we both
have "I's."
          You do not know who "I" am.
How could you?
The "I" is apart from anything
that I can say about it.
I do not know you.
You are other.
We're each other's other.
Let's stay that way.
This language is in between
me and you, separating us.
Yes, we all shake our heads in unison.
We understand, not each other.

10.

This should happen every day, because I want it to, because
we all enjoy similar things, because if it does happen I will let
my body be used in any way the other wants to use it, I am at
their will, and in this exchange of wills, beauty can exist. My
will desires this, and will and desire are everything. I need a
steady diet of fresh bodies, and you do too. We all need this
friendship, this bond. There are no real bonds except this
one.

QUARTET
(for Dominique Lowell)

part one

I survive alone in this bizarre territory
by my stubborn kicks in this city of yes
this empty apartment of uh-huh or this bar of maybe
well, maybe there's honey in this pocket of sweat
I emerge a brand new baby from ashes of last night
one more than one too many thorns
I wonder if this squeaky casino has a Xerox machine
available?
I feel him in my throat and want to choke up the vomit
I want to cross a river by intuition and the use of vines
praise the function of my organs
how they work together in unison
that's beauty, Tom Dooley
they don't shut down at two o'clock
that's the "go on" and the "push" in me
praise the way beer floats down the river of my heart
when no man has the guts to go
my heart needs lubrication though
the zoo of me and you has no bars
to keep us from destroying each other
the pain of yes,
the deep cut of uh-huh
the fucked-up shitfaced of maybe
in my movie I may or may not make a cameo

you're a big pain in the neck
actually a big fucking headache
and when I get a massage each worry appears in bold
Technicolor
like some old forgotten boyfriend who I remembered to
forget about
if you are the hurt, it doesn't hurt enough
I want to get off too
you don't deserve to be a pain in my neck
so get out of there and buy me some aspirin

I will never let you occupy my dreams
or have a role in them unless you have a note from your
mother
saying you're not a total asshole

twist my arms, wrap my legs
enter my veins, consume
the flesh that cover my bones
I'm banging my head against the wall
and the pain is not going away
it's not going away
not going away

part two

I got to do something about this weather
I'm changing the sun and the moon
make it go away
make it into a movie about my life that never was
my movie has a good ending
but you're going to have to wait
because we're in a long line
without any cigarettes
I don't care about that
I'm only getting nearer to death
and I'm in no hurry
it's the driest fuck that I worry about
but that's a complaint directed towards God
and not you

kiss my ass, little surfer girl
and fuck those cars that speed up
on Howard street while I'm crossing
it's time for change
and it's always that time
but change comes from within
my life on foot in my worn shoes

I'm aware of many times

118

I was in that dream reading this poem
and I have many uses and know
the many uses of the asshole
so what?

oh no!
it's the beginning of another day
what a drag
I drag my bones through time
things are going constantly in and out of my body
that is the interesting part
the bad part is that which only bruises me
but I can take it
I know your name
do I?

part three

"there is a lot of water here"
a quart of beer and a cigarette
this is the world according to me
the radio on only one frequency
your mind needs a new battery
my cough is swinging with new diseases
so stay away and go away
a few vitamins is all it takes
to get me in the confessional mood
do you have a light?
notice how I'm gathering momentum
my friends are a singing people
in leather thrones carrying big whips
they have a metallic look to them
and like to watch the canal traffic going by
in other words, you're fucked
I voted for a pot smoker this year
next year I will vote for a cocksucker
"yes, I sucked his cock but I didn't swallow"
this is the world according to me
in my movie there is a big fat cock

and a big fat pussy
that's all the plot that I need
your eyes look like mercury
and there's too much water in this beer
a 40 ouncer in my lap
not a drop of sperm in it
sperm that is as foreign as mercury to me
this is the world according to me

part four

fairly white yes
and dripping
sifting through dried blood
with its dripping seal of approval
I hesitate in the subway
I sense a disaster involving potato chips
I used to not believe in magic
except when its terror stabs at me
with quick glimpses of yesterdays
and empty pockets
I'm not your girl machine
girl machine, girl machine
play that record again
yes fairly white stop

SONNETS

Bright the money zilch
Could happen to you I
Am still waiting for you to
Sneeze say "pleeze"
Out of the xerox machine
And now you're off the rocks
Is it true? No, no new
The fire the fireworks look out!
And look at it all zooming
Pre-fuck and post-clothed
Check the bob hobnobbing
With the nelly waiter
Open someone else's letters
And live look for security

Bare branches filled with snow
Ice all over the ground
Faces covered the concept of subways
Graffiti in the Lower East Side
All over the walls fires on
Houston Street boats in the East river
Subway token empty buildings
The story goes on a reinforcement
Something to drink should I return to the penthouse
Where is it to where?
Sunday morning Bowery prostitutes
Chinatown Canal Street
Graffiti on Bowery prostitutes
3rd Street and 6th Avenue

Under telegraph wires
Sodden rye baked red
Tin gongs sawblades
Flatten its frosted snout
Whistle blast first place
Last breath remove the head gear
Play the decadent epigram
lozenges and the skeleton

In shadow less than blue grass
Scribbled visible
Silver less interior
Little brown shoe echoes
Wings increase its loaf
A mattress of thought

I'm like a one-legged man
at an ass-kicking, you're
like a defeated chess-player.
You feel raped, but I'm tired.
I annoyed you and you
write about it; I give you
all your good lines. I'm good with
the stick, what can I say?
Hello, mom, how's it going?
I like my phrase better
than that word that you choose.
Oops! Spoon it out, by the pound,
and let me have a lick.
No spoon? Or fork?

Magnitude miraculously
Variations human "I read you"
Strain longest cab elevation
Millions rapid motion infinite
Identity specific notion junk-bond
Robber baron flew the coop
Free trade aging realists
Taxes sand black with soot
Surgery what hat with ribbons?
Massive overall miracles
Oracles passing trade bunk
"You need me" little Bo Peep
A rubber suit bum level freeze
Uniform baby goo goo glow in the dark

Spare invisible skate toilet
Militant scream vandalize
Terrorist grocery store wall

Of carrots sandbag lettuce
Martyr wanted FDA zucchini
Bushels dish mish-mash hot
Milk gas school history
Church landfill free invisible
Wall mall fall doll go media
Together bugs sweating vinegar
biological date kingdom whopping
Pot tidbits bitten off
Spread rage news secrets lie
Known own up social scandal

The bus terminals resemble
each other all around the world
In a flash we descend on Cleveland
The lights the lights the
City is dead, no one awake
after two o'clock
I take two photographs of
abandoned Pasadena or Santa Ana
The suburban charm
The discreet no wonder the Browns
were lousy last year
Television cost a quarter so
I will not watch it
The same floors in every airport sleeplessness

Peace rap rupture text pot top
Bye twang twang bingo bang
Bob good to see you bob Bob?
Get out the Monopoly board
I love you the things I do
For you you scatterbrain
Lame brain hey I'm lame too
I'm good at backgammon
I double you built like Wilt
I need another leg Mom stole
One where's all the money honey?
No honey no home built like
A castle with pink walls frosting

A high paying job I hate it

I'm broke. Some friends
are sleeping on the couch.
I haven't paid the rent yet.
So far, this month I am
doing better. I'm hanging
out in some South of Market
café, which I rarely do.
I'm selling some books.
Scraping up money for coffee.
Everything is going soon at
this rate. Everything will
go out the door. I'm just
trying not to get kicked out
of the apartment.

Soy bean hot sauce drink
It's good it's better than
My last girlfriend
Don't talk like that bow down
I have to go meet somebody
Just after seeing a beauty
She's around the corner crush
Drink your soup shut trap
Fender bender poetry which
Seems like battered children
I slap the world revenge
We're in an S & M exchange
Right now that's OK
I'm human created equal

No dreams about people
All the trust is gone
Satie in the background
A contract
Is there something happening here
that I don't know about?
I've been there in Williamsburg
I was twelve years old

The first time I saw Cézanne
There are no problems
Only opportunities
Hold all the paintings up
Behind the car
The Brooklyn Public Library

The rosy fingers of dawn
Slept in today this morning
No lines to wait in
Wrote a few letters last night to the
Brooklyn duo Grose/Brunak
They make little sense
But spatially they're interesting
Some woman walks
Across the room
It garners my attention
Others talk the many Carlas that live on Polk street
I'm reading "The Golden Ass"
That wakes me up today
My article in The Bay Guardian

Woman with pierced nose long hair
My stomach hurts
Limps across the room where's Snow?
I adhere to the lines
I smell turpentine
Forgot to call my mother last night
Donald Grose lives in Brooklyn
Everything is flashing lights
I do not know the zip code
Everyone erases this is not poetry
Just some notes I write like I haven't
Written for the last few months
Poetry
Contest

I've just won say again
From Motherlode to Edinburgh
I see Avery "hello" and

Order an Irish coffee
I'm with Kathi Georges and Kip
We're drinking holidays
More beer that's the guy from
Faith No More over there
I'm a fraud though but that's
Alright "I'm a nice guy"
In the "fuck you" generation
I'm not really a nice guy
"Fuck you" I will kill you
Get out of my face

In forty years when you are very old,
wrinkles and dark circles under your eyes,
how you are now, young, will be no longer.
Your beauty will not be a young beauty.
Someone will ask "where did your beauty go?"
Can you remember those days of pleasure?
I can see in those eyes of yours, nothing
but those spendthrift manners and empty words.
Maybe you would still be beautiful this
day if you had a son and a husband
and an old love still as fierce and strong, and then
all beauty would belong to more than you.
You will remember these words when you are
old, when a living heart will have then died.

I'm witnessing the death of
San Francisco as an entity.
I'm dying because of the
Marxist angle and the
communal marketing technique.
Your social realism dulls
my hopes of fantasy and imagination.
Man. I know it's bleak,
but I don't want to dwell
in the shit. I can only think
of somewhere else or someone
else. My desire right now
is important, not the

harmony of the planet. It's
time to think small.

Bare branches filled with snow
Ice all over the ground
Faces covered the concept of subways
Graffiti in the Lower East Side
Everything is flashing lights
I do not know the zip code
Everyone erases this is not poetry
each other all around the world
In a flash we descend on Cleveland
The lights the lights the
wrinkles and dark circles under your eyes,
how you are now, young, will be no longer.
Your beauty will not be a young beauty.
But spatially they're interesting

I'm listening to the most
pathetic conversation in this city.
I'm sitting here and
listening to this shit, I am
writing about it, and I am
talking about it. Talk
about boring, this is it.
It's raining outside. I'm taking it
easy, my legs are tired from
running. Shit, legs, shitting.
This is San Francisco, and
I'm in it. I'm on it.
Sitting in the chair. Simone is
waiting for me. Laughter.

Things take a while hey
If I stayed here last year
In San Francisco things
Would have been different
Get him on the phone and
I'm always on the phone

Talked to Stephanie Phillips yesterday
She will come to America soon
Steve Brown lives here as well
I saw him last night
With a strange-looking haircut
I have his phone number
And now Terry Wood has moved in
I found a place to live too

I've been sleeping a lot
Lately Otter and I
Went to go get some pizza
It's cold in my room
Otter was dressed as a boy scout
Fist up her pussy
Meeting with Rita Ricardo
That night we went to The End Up
We meet Donald and others
I give Otter a buttrub
Rex is on the phone
And one day we will all get fangs
It rains like no rain ever
Let it rain on my house

Koo carrot-top claws
Had scuffed tortoise agreed
A skull scumbled with calcium
Inscribed a number naked
Under their blue guillotine
Blade voice amid the rabble
Bleeding necklaces belly and
Bones with the effeminate body
Burgeoning mustache barefoot
For symmetry's sake some
Arsonist a lackey comparable
To the jellyfish supple leather
Blistering the heel brown
Prison-like blankets feathers

Boy, are my roots killing me.

I don't trust that dog.
It's not easy being greenery.
Look, a walking cactus.
Flattery will get you nowhere, babe.
I guess you can go
back to your Editor jobs.
This cactus plant slays me.
Anything for a laugh.
Eat some paste.
It's okay. That
was years ago.
You can drop me
at the bar, please.

Street chalk system koo
Hourglass settles blimp
Dust breathe interception
Entrance facade zing
Movie threat feed pot
Homeless beep beep
Porn love housing complex
Boot Jack shuffle board
Old maid lust
Walker talker
IV boo natural neutral
Zero green xerox
On ice
Butt rub jack plug
Hear me need need

DOUBLE BREASTED JOKE
(for Charles Allen Jones)

I was once a clown in a carnival and I traveled all through the United States.

Marilyn Monroe was once engaged to Albert Einstein.

A drunk man balances his double vision by walking horizontal.

San Francisco is a ghost town.

When you get to Geary Street go right.

When you get to Jones Street go sinister.

To write like Charles Bukowski, you must drink gin and bourbon and whatever else everyday for twenty-five years.

The government should take money away from the military and invest it in liver transplant research.

Robert Mapplethorpe was the second coming of Christ but no one noticed.

I met him once in New York City and took his photograph.

All lines will converge someday.

Who was breast-fed and who wasn't?

Everyone here is insane.

Choose from the above.

Take your pick.

JOSEPH BEUYS IN BERLIN

Joseph, wake up!
Joseph wakes up.
Where is Germany, Joseph?
Where are all the women,
and men, and the children?

Nothing is ugly!

In your dream
Wagner spoke to you.
He asked "What happened?"

The world is composed of materials.
To live is to be an artist.

In your dream
Germany spoke to you.

No one is not an artist:
everyone is an artist.

Joseph, wake up!

I cannot be myself without my hat.
I cannot think without my hat.
I cannot create without my hat.
I may run for a political office.

Germany is destroyed.
Germany is silence.
We have inherited a past
that none of us want,
that none feels responsible for.

But what then have we inherited?
Silence, burning buildings, corpses, and guilt.
This is Germany now.

We are not the judges.
We are only the judged.
We have to live under pressure.

I cannot say that word.
I cannot breathe.
I am drowning.

Der Rhine!
The ghosts of the past are hiding
in Berlin's sewage.
I will search for them.

It is not a crime
to be a German.
Be quiet, Joseph!
They are watching!

Goethe, Wagner, Hegel, and Rilke.
Beethoven, Bach, Schopenhauer, and Hoffmann.

Wake up, Joseph!
Here's your hat!

My heritage and your heritage.
Where is it now?

Excerpt from unfinished poem
THE WILL TO POWER

liberate the "anonymity of the work"
we test the eternal return
multiple modes of folding up
origins (oppressive weather)
event or task of pre-sensing
the finite thinking of returning
"perfection is finite" movement
new score order
"rescind" on my convictions
today is August, 1881
loss? gain? my turn?

sticky   (it)   struck   (it)   secrecy
                        failure
voodoo's belly-dance, smile's boot
unraveling fingers in scatter
lights glare eternal single file
automobile's pre-sensing
slavery   caution ahead, poets at
work the knives are bloody
buzzing modes of fireball
6000 feet beyond man
"it invaded me"

TSZ

possible thought of a possibility
struggle program "thunder-ball"
flux atomic forces
flowing with the flux of becoming
forming the "ation"
the demonstration   fast-forward
thinking/knowing

not making claims for the truth
modesty/rigor
not making claims for animals
the experimentation of trans-human
test drive (return of the ghosts)
Today mostly everything is
the Nietzsche test drive

piety but also anarchy
return of rope
also Hitchcock's fax
failure of man's custodianship
"have we cleaned the world's
toilet bowl enough today?"
scandal of reference
am I referring to anything?
when entering the metaphysical
impulse (on the scale, heartbeat)
check the biological cause
need medicine

his protocols turn into
"I didn't mean it"
look at the horizon of doom
how the rope comes together
perfect murder transmission
crypt gathering magnetized

"Today everybody is....
for him or against him"
luminous moments
that we only contain
mostly jailed Mozart

absence of work
series of moments

temporal closure problems
fine tuned ears of finitude
signatures (homeless referent)
today
everybody is
for Wagner's
corpse buried under the table
we eat our dinner
the name "vertigo" 50-50

JAM THE CODES!

E-MAIL KISSES

lost object, failed scents
hunger's annihilation of property
gangster theory versus production
apple cores / signed masks
good acts of violence
common cause versus
separate texts individuate
mourning material objects
VERTIGINOUS COMMANDS
"We're not going to clear his name"
            critical mass truth polls
drama of failed maternal apples
impossible odor rendez-vous

JE SUIS FEMME
conversation with an otherness
dialectical third term of infinity
F/M pact with established regression
may my existence be stylized
throwing up life's parasitical logic
it's easier to live without movement

having four stomachs ruminating

                    BREAK
ejected cyst / foreign body origin
kill off the despair tract ^^^ nausea

          this is a haunted epoch

Book Five: Alphabet Cities (1990)

A FILM THAT MARILYN MONROE
NEVER MADE

In the story
M was the
last revolutionary.

She was a
Mexican communist
and most called
her "Mama."

A leader
was assassinated
and M
was thrown
in jail.

She did not kill
the man, but
her lover
was death.

Many years
passed.
During a
civil war
M escaped
from prison

but no one
ever knew
what happened
to her.

BENTE MOONE

Every dog has a tale to tell.
The cosmos? Feldspar?
Energy. Agate lamp of / radar arrange
How do I introduce the freak?
Flecks of the crystal.
Picking up the song leaves
and the dust. Along the moors.
I am a joker
in your pack of cards.
Gravity. Cobra. Dome.
I am a purr boxer
in your carton thoughts of England.
The moon
is a punching bag.
No, it isn't!
It is a pugilist
with a glass jaw.
I want to punch it
and knock it out.

BODY

I start anew, the triple exposure, blurred photography where clapping means little, and polite laughter is a balloon that pops. I can imagine my face in the other person's mind, but what face is it? I do not understand you. We hurt each other often, sometimes with fiction. Sometimes with bricks. How do you understand those distant places? They battle, but it's not our battle. We only understand winner and losers. I wake up, turn on the radio, wait. I turn on the hot water, and wait. Only this time the pain is real. It is difficult. I do not know how two people can arrange a meeting. Accidental arrangement. This conversation includes everybody, so join in when you want to. Someone I know is boarding a plane to Amsterdam.

The human body purged totally purged its appetites, desires.
Body passage. Seemingly.
Passions and vices, admiration of the vulgar shit,
oral, face to face, serene composure.
Sensual fuck, tyranny fuck.
Voracious hi-fi record of Nancy Sinatra singing
"Sundown, Sundown"
rising above the body of nails.
Table shriek, puppet's deliberate goal, shit.
Absolutely itself, fluidity. Breeze, balance soft
and melodious flow, arrest it. International charity,
hurricane excess, symbiotic contact.
Body fruitful, female age of green reproduction.
Dentistry result: self-created pain.
Victim's lament overshadowing their bodies.
Rooted age. Another's skin rigid, self-convoluting,
prolonged in butterfly eyelashes. Benign.
Heard fantasy truly clean.
A smile few count: student soil.
Elderly supplanting. Build, build. Lacquered
Japanese boxes and then went down to the ship.
Abundant wine breaks ill-fate. From sunburned,
page 275, start sucking nipples. Chokes, hits,
the cat, back of fucking neck. Ointment.

Lick her cunt, the unique, palace in smoky light.
I rape her weekend, all of it, I want all of it!
Visit me. Get to the pool, our savior, the pool.
Take the doors off quick. Strange smell turns
into a motorcycle. Slap Godzilla, slap the asshole,
slap your mother, slap your identity, throw yourself out.
Back at the hotel, in front of the TV.

I am searching. I left the car. I've left her. They are in the
back seat. It's time to find him. I've come here to meet him.
He sends me a messenger. His name is Jacques. He brings
me a can of tuna. He is guilty of a voracious orality. Don't
say anything. I zip up my zipper. Speechless. Searching for
him. I left them for a reason. We talk about my favorite book
"The Great Fire of London." A book by Clifford Irving.
The next day a letter came. Unexpected. "I never did it in a
Volvo." He has no property, he drifts. I zip up the search.
Bob sees me. He joins me. Eclipse.

The black and gold bottle shaped into an owl said "Made in
Lyon." The note inside is forged. All about friendship that I
question now. I had a brief conversation with the gay eel,
and it reported the facts about how to suck a breast. Once a
daughter. And you know how the body can change shapes:
can you follow the transformations? Boy, was that a steep
symphony that I just dove into. I stuck out my hand out of
the water and a dream ends. Say "hey" when you touch
bodies beneath the waist. Look up, and look out for water. I
learned that dance from those weird Incas. The fat is gone.
Centerless. You have to be in touch with your roots. Watch
out, this body will tear easy.

Rise and die. Slide down that silver spike whistle. The
children I left behind sleep here. Your favorite dish. I made it
especially for you. Elaine's legs are all that's wrong with her.
Have you gambled away the money your father gave which
I'd dropped into my pocketbook? Spilled a lot of impressive
scenery, almost lost food of childhood. Pastel sketches of
shepherds, as they float home, and haul them in. His aches,
German songs he sang in the bath, but let's bury them

together anyway. Why did her mouth make me remember
things? Why do children burrow in dirt? She was something,
like the sky, I never saw enough of.

CROCODILES

A dark shape. Look at the cups,
the bricks, the lines of children,
and try to find their significance.

We are unable. Their significance
escapes us. Cups, bricks, lines of children.
Let them be, they can never mean.

Look at the cups, bricks, lines of children,
not for their significance, but for what they are.
What they are is not what they mean.

Crocodiles. Damn them! What are they? Ugly?
Look at them! You know what they are. I have
seen a crocodile. No, I haven't.

DEMOCRACY

30 billion dollars of profit, and possibly
we should take a position on the subject of prostitution.
The n is an insect which lands on an orange,
a poet once told me in a dark recess of an institution.
Lands of orange trees.
An object of prostitution.
The poet once told me.
We should take a position. Can we?
This leveling may be fun.
The poet cannot profit.
The word "profit" does not exist in South America.
A big zero.
We are near a lake taking off our shirts
getting ready for a brief swim.
An hour before I read a note which Tama sent me.
The water is still, and the big cities do not mind
partial nudity, a reference to the imperial,
yet the cabin was left unlocked
because of your indifference.
We are all saddened by the death of Francis Ponge.
You advised me politely: "take what you want."
Your portrayal suggested that there is
nothing, nothing that you would die over.
She said "black is a universal color."
But I thought black was not a color and told her so.
"The universe is black, black like the universe."
Her gesture had attached aristocratic tendency.
Working classes demand their streets back.
I know ever since reproduction that neither you nor I
are attached to anything.
Then destructive motives become our best intentions.
Only life is what we must hold on to,
until they are able to clone us:
waking us up from the deep freeze.
When us dead awaken and honest doctors
give everyone, including Walt,
new life and new jobs by
giving us new legs and new hearts.
Will the factory take me?

HAIKUS

MY FRIEND IS FAT

Every year he gains
fifty pounds. One day as big
as the room he is.

ACCIDENT

Someone rearranged
the furniture. During night
I go pee. Stub toe.

ACCIDENT #2

He bumped me. I bumped
the baby carriage. The bus did
not stop. Look out! Shit!

ACCIDENT #3

"Don't worry, it's a
BB gun." Boy points it at
my face. Lucky day.

I WENT TO BED WITH MARCIA BRADY

Of all my years and
lovers, she understood me.
Marcia was fifteen.

GERMAN ROOMMATES

They didn't pay off
the phone bills, rent, and they left
a phony address.

SEQUEL

I don't understand
Germans. We speak English but
don't communicate.

JE SUIS LE LIVRE

Je suis le livre
que je parle.

The hidden quality in this angle.
That something always hides
at each moment
and nothing comes over
with clarity and fullness.

When you speak I shall take
your words with care.
I will give you silence and seriousness,
and you too can stretch out
and relax in this ideal living room.

There will always be some
cold drinks in the refrigerator.
When I turned away from yourself
but was still aware that you were there.

I was trying to experience it all,
every aspect of life, and by doing so,
I forgot you for
a moment.

LAUGHED, DRANK, AND WENT DOWN
IN A TAILSPIN

Whoever you are, you have created the world.
And if you are the creator, that troubles me.
It's not that you are a bad person, or insensitive,
it's just because I hardly know you.

No one listen to the poet anymore,
screaming his lungs out on the street.
The inner world has disappeared and got a job.
My manifestos and notes have been ignored.

Listen to the entirety. Whoever you are,
and wherever you come from is unimportant.
Some of us wear masks, and drink too much,
and most of us are too tired and hungry.

Ballantine ale and solitaire every day
of your life: your life in which you kept quiet.
In those times which you should show more reserve
to someone else, and in those times where your mind
tells you, you should, and everyone is much happier.
"There is a seriousness to anything which is said"
she said. And across the wall in the bathroom you
signed your name next to hers, and someone knocked
on the door because you were taking too long.

First, I said, That I would be arriving,
but never came, and to my disappointment
followed other's disappointments.

To smash and to break the rock
into little pieces, so that you do
not remember why you did it.
We all paid homage to her beauty
which we were reminded of nightly.
It was as if she took off her clothes
and walked around the house every evening,
later, going to the refrigerator

to get some ice cream.

His voice was completely audible
although I could never remember what
he said in the dark.
John McCormack entertained me
when I was younger.
Old records that were part of my parents'
record collection.

If there was blue, it was announced previously,
and this blue continued on and ended in some river.
The telephone and the conversations we had, the endless
late night conversations we had.

All of us had them in that era.
I was surprised to find a phone jack in my bedroom.
In that era, every meeting we had, on the phone,
or in real life, was a surprise.

M (The Blue Notebook 1990)

1.   M

It's dark (empty) and no one is close to us. Scotoma, are you
listening to rueful bicycles in the night? I cannot sleep and I
move closer to you. Caution. Can you hear my blunt voice in
the night? My neon body is against yours broken yellow, this
day has ended stranded. Are you sleeping like an envelope in
the night, Mr Carpenter?

2.   MM

Joseph Beuys in the red sofa, sofa larva next to the felt
billboard, next to you waft. The phrase was spoken bulk in
tongue hiatus, I took it thudding seriously. I said sapphire. I
wish that I didn't say anything. I take it back. Then lemon
phrase when floral dress disappears. Flutes exchanged. The
white and black memory remnant doesn't help. No change
apparent. Cats disappearing. Men honks arriving on wires
airplanes. All contained in this painting cylinder. The table
arrived in the mail. Traveling men in jumpsuits. Awl vortex
gasket fossil. My favorite color? Minette's favorite: green.
Mine: permanent red! I take it all back, all, all, back....

3.   MMM

Thursday geyser morning: I will worship The Butthole
Surfers. Not really floor. Or space. Saturday: more travelers,
more humidity Saturdays. I think of the day when we will be
getting to each other. Stepping in the shoes of no one. I am
'eaking to your 'ents in 'tish 'umbia. They are umbra gods. I
sit in back the theater and blinded. Tears never shelved
solved my suds problems. You are another mist person,
reminded of this viper notion daily. We could be thumb kids.
Monica face the gloam hospital. I will cirrus visit her.
Coinage. The hammer goes boom!

4.   MMMM

Your face becomes hair dimmer in my flask mind, Taylor,
always thinking of other sedimentary things. I do not watch
much caterpillars on television selling me war and I hope
bleeding to remember each moment sitcom well. I do not
ask "what do you think?" (of rotten denmark flesh) but want
to know anyway. I never have the nerve engine to ask you
these questions rearrange and my loaf curiosity is always
being tickled. I walk down berry the streets like Fillmore and
Pierce or wherever they always fade speak of you, you oiled
butt walking somewhere, being some(no)where vague hole
harp, sometimes with other people ants, sometimes with me.

5.   MMMMM

"Trotsky met me in Mexico today, by shred ship, he came
moldy on the Ruth. The sun blazing on oil baked skins." His
white insect hair in Mexico. The waves ruffle off the coast.
His brown suit of care. My birthday is over torn and I did
not grid enjoy it that much. I enjoyed myself a few days
around my worn birthday when I was celebrating with Dave
Harding, but when I got back to hole San Francisco, did not
corn click. There was an uneasiness, candles. This year will
allow dangled change. That's OK. My grandfather died on
my birth(death)day this lethal year. I am still thinking
obliquely what that means. His death and the loss of other
friends. Nerve flakes, sucking crayon.

6.   MMMMMM

I talk and it seems that we're not even speaking the same
language. If I ever thought I had it all figured out, what a
laugh, I'm way off! There's always something going on that's
not a part of me, the foreign element, that I do not know
about. I'm missing out on something somewhere. I thought
that I was clear about it all. No one feels the same way that I
do. Hey, I do not understand you. But that's fine. Who does?
You have created a vicious space to live in, and I want to
penetrate that space.

7.   MMMMMMM

I have you in my balanced arms now and I will always equate
you have you. Equating it with it and you, and the missing
letters. It is meaningful to me, and yet I do not know what it
means. That's all we get in this hostile life.
       A brief moment, then....

A strange pink vision of beauty comes to park mind, pack
unclear, diction undefined.

8.   MMMMMMMM

The splinter field of the sleeping alphabet breaks open the
conclusion. No end to this city vision part dream part real.
Your drift vulnerable position makes you choke semantically
on your verbs. My vulnerable position makes me
unprotected from you, shaken by the cityscape I have lost my
tongue weapons.

9.   MMMMMMMMM

Perjury? How could you? Could you? "...." The lemon phrase
floral disappears. Flutes memory remnant change apparent
disappearing. Men honks wires airplanes

10.   MMMMMMMMMM

Monica is sick of vowels and I will take care of her.
I will bring her something to drink and some medicine.
I will cure her. Later, I will go to the supermarket

and will buy her some groceries.
We will talk about things and will touch each other.
We will embrace each other.
We will be next to each other in (coffined) bed.

11.   MMMMMMMMMMM

You are not here right now and I am alone with this
breathing pen and blank piece of growing paper. Your feast
absence opens the door to sponge memory, and I want to
enjoy and view your vanilla presence, now somehow blacker
and dimmed, but sometimes vivid as in destitute dreams. I
am the worst judge of memories and what dreams mean, but
your bright face burns in my mind and that illuminated
knowledge satisfies my dark hunger temporarily, and teases
me for not only an appearance but an embrace more real
than dreams. I speak in a forbidden area, I make myself
vulnerable, my feelings opens wide: I speak only to you.
What I like best about you is the sound of your voice, and
when you call me at night, afterwards I sleep much better.
Your cold voice enters the energy of my being mysteriously.
Wherever you are, you seem much closer. Sometimes I like
the feeling of love, that high, more than you. I do not want
to possess an image of you, but you, nightly, in some
crepuscular room.

12.   MMMMMMMMMMM

I have all these photographs of you. Is everything a
substitute for something else? Is everyone a substitute for
someone else? I want to be a substitute for myself.

13.   MMMMMMMMMMM

I don't know what will happen to us,
the past renewed and the present are unclear.
My beliefs are not without fear attached,
and that's not a problem.
Who has a heart that does not oscillate
between those distant cities of yes and no?
Besides M?
I accept that you have disappeared
and that you are death.

Even with harsh knowledge pressing,
I will hope for the best, and make
a blind thrust in your direction.
Missing, missing, but I have to leave,
and you could be anyone.

MM

We spent so many quiet days, and so many hectic hours
knowing nothing of the complex ideas of philosophy. Later
we had to read many books by Marshall McLuhan. I looked
forward to the bright day when I could wake up and take a
walk during early spring without many concerns. A subtle
walk in the parks of my dreams on the west side of the city,
and stay there all day to watch the sun go down eventually.
Nightfall. Crystal flags....

You used to watch sunsets, remember?
It's so late now, that M
has departed to New York City.
She has taken up residence in
the lower east side (loisaida)
where she has
become an underground writer.
She hasn't written often to me
and she never calls.
I drove her to the airport
where I last saw her.
She left so many memories
and her clothes are still in the closet.
Should I sell them?
She used to know many people here;
she introduced me to many friends over the years.
Her name comes up in conversation less and less.

He asked me "did Georges
Bataille and Marcel Mauss
ever meet?" I didn't know
and had given up my job
as a research librarian months ago.
Now, all I wanted to do was
solve crossword puzzles and
make visits to South America.
All I wanted to know was
did Marcel Mauss and Marilyn Monroe
ever meet? Or did Marcel Mauss and
Marshall McLuhan ever meet? Mickey
Mouse never entered the picture.

Thanks for letting me sleep
on your bed. I hadn't had
any rest for a week
and here it is so warm.
In the morning I will make you
some coffee and break open some
mussel shells for breakfast.
There were a few phone calls
for you last night.
Did you enjoy the play?
I didn't do very much last night.
I read, and I listened to the radio,
smoked a few cigarettes,
and then fell asleep. My grandmother's
birthday is coming up, you know.

The czar wept anew when
the dune buggy suffered from boils.
On beaches we stay too long and
leave with sun-burnt backs, and return
home where we find a cure
in the form of some inexpensive lotion.
After returning from my vacation,
I inherited a pile of letters.

One from Marilyn which she
must have sent many months ago.
She writes: "I'm tired of being
noticed and have resorted to
hiding out in cheap hotels."
She left no return address.

I once saw Mickey Mantle
hit a grand slam at Yankee Stadium
and I called it "Impossible Action Painting."
It was like Abstract Expression in that
Clete Boyer, Bobby Richardson, and
Billy Martin were on base.
I had just bought two giant hot dogs
and a large beer, very cheap back then.
I was sitting in the right field bleachers.
It was a 2-2 fastball.
I heard a crack of a bat.
It was a towering shot
towards me, the right fielder
crashed against the wall.
I dropped my beer and hot dogs,
and they landed on the right fielder,
and I caught the ball.

I dream of Van Gogh or Cézanne, all their paintings were
erased or destroyed. I dream of George once: what was he
doing though? I dream that I was still in high school, but
why do I never dream that I am in college? I was on a bus
going to high school with my friend, George, and we were
talking about Van Gogh or Cézanne, or some painter. Later,
when I started to go to college, I met another person named
George who hated Van Gogh.

The buses stopped
when Ludwig Wittgenstein
walked across Market Street.
He did not know the meaning of "red."
He never wrote a book.
Some suffer in the university.
Some wish to be dead in an auto accident.
I saw a one-legged man
die on Turk Street.

Eagle, Buddha with wings.
Lion, wholly destructive
but creative as well.
Snake, a desert coil.
M is the 13th letter of the alphabet.
There is no 13th Avenue in San Francisco.
M has two humps like a camel.
"Do you have a cigarette?"
Shut up!

These are the memoirs of
a Marilyn Monroe impersonator:
"I am in my late thirties now,
and was an impersonator for most
of my adult life.
I lived in and around Hollywood.
I worked in Las Vegas for a
few years, and the money was good.
There were some difficult years though.
I was abused by my boyfriend and had
a serious drug problem for many years.
I felt exploited by some of the men
that I worked for, and I was raped a few times.
Now, I do not work much, but I have
enough money to live comfortably."

How's your ass?
The tattoo is almost done by now.
The books are due
at the North Beach Library.
They've issued a death warrant.
You are a dead man.
I used your ID post-death.
You drink Campari
at Savoy Tifoli.
Are you from Burlingame?
1891-1944

This is Brautigan Street--
all the trees are bare.
There is a French bakery.
Most the stores are empty.
Brautigan is not dead.
He went to China
many years ago and
has never come back.
I think he's staying.
He got a haircut
and became a Maoist.
Today, I live in his
old room in North Beach.
I guess Grant Street
is not good enough for him!

This is best expressed in mime.
All my confessions.
Why are you silent?
Why do I project
these long pauses?
I am not Marcel Marceau, thank God!
I am not a member of the Mime Troupe.
We have nothing to say
to each other.
Do you have a tool?

Something to break the ice?
Something to stop
the silence?

Imagine a place without
final surfaces, endless
shapes that replace
each other, and you
cannot grasp any one
of them. A place where
everyone can drink a
serious dark beer when
dying of thirst. Water
floods my bed and the lands
and it revives the trees and
everything. No final bodies,
no places to rest your mind.
You are not the end
of you.

"Love is no way to treat a friend." Not even in China. So do
not try to fool me with all your intellectual digressions. I was
very happy till you came along. You who are also me. I had a
philosophy that I could live with: a way of life. And you
came with all your problems and troubles. I do not need the
drama.

Our life is the most intense
rendez-vous ever of
words and things.
Boys have become
flowers and words.
Flowers become boats
on rivers, stones become fish.
Corpses become trees,
and trees become men.
Men make houses and books,

women sing and have children.
Animals run and look for food.
All these words and things
and nothing stopping them.

Collecting darkness for
a future rummage sale.
All the old oddities
out of the closet.
Life is a deadly
white noise, Rex told me.
Nothing is beginning
or ending.
It just goes on.
Life is an endless
sax solo.
Can you imagine it?
The endless orgy.
Why so depressed?

It's
March, mussels, madness,
mind, matter, mass,
mountains, Mars, moments,
motion, mother.
Mind, memory, Mary Magdalene,
ministers, mince pie,
mammary glands.
Mambo, mambo,
mama mia,
missing, maybe, might,
modern, molecules.
Me, my, maybe.

Here's the ideal team:
Ezra "the dog" Pound, first base
Jack "Jack" Spicer, second base

Gilbert "Gil" Sorrentino, third base
W. C. "Doc" Williams, shortstop
Frank "Lana" O'Hara, left field
Arthur "Rainbow" Rimbaud, center field
S. "the diceman" Mallarmé, right field
Charles "Goodtime Charlie" Baudelaire, the pitcher
Richard "mayonnaise" Brautigan, catcher
You couldn't lose!

Flowers are actors.
Put them in a sand pail.
All the world's a stage.
Put them in a vase.
Make a painting.
Put them in a grave.
They are dying.
Put them so that
they form the letter "M."
Hooray for Hollywood.

MYTH OF THE GERBIL

In the beginning there was the gerbil.

Red crimson. Tantalizing wanton inviting gerbil.
Brightness of air. No illusions. Mother, father, gerbil.
Grey sunset. Light of the first sun, gerbil.
Accepting orifice of gerbil.
Holes deep and deeper, horrified accounts.
Wanting warm womb of mother gerbil.
Lips of death, kiss of sugar, gerbil.

Brave gerbil, ejaculation. Industry gerbil. Seedy liquid.
Commercial gerbil. A depiction of yggdrasil in a seventeen-
century Icelandic manuscript by gerbil. No names please.
Method actor in leopard's eyes, gerbil. Silverfish, houseguest:
planet of gerbils. Earth crawling with seeds. Your seeds.
Confused ruse of gerbil, also known as "jerboa," snakelike.

I am the gerbil who lives in Peru.
The fly in the ointment.
Out of my eyes, damn seed!
Green trunk of secrets.
We'll always hold it against you.

Boa constrictor gulping down a cheese danish. Oval orange
vertebrae branching off, the trees of family gerbil. Young
hard sprucebuds. Alter-ego gerbil. Kissed dandelion-caps.
Super-ego, irises in bee-meadow gerbil. Tidal lagoon next to
grassy bluff, blue-faced, eyesockets of skull, gerbil. Green
grown teeth hear the prayer of yellow-eyed gerbil.

Cloud-shadow and anonymous sex partners
via glory hole, or an alley
"I do know who you are."

Warm liquid, and then darkness of gerbil consciousness.

Church of glorious gerbil,
hair grows, falls.
Gold light pierced her eyes through the oak trees.
Giant red plastic gerbil bought by a tourist.
Calliope of metal and ghosts.
Nostrils drink the sublime bowels of the city.
The fading moment of the final, last gerbil.

PANGRAMS

1.
Jump over the bowl
of borscht, quiz me,
vile zebra.
Fix the wings that
glide.
The kangaroo yawns.

2.
A whisper zigzags from
X to the egg's yolk.
A V.W. is burnt.
Midday crisis
in joining the queue.

3.
The telephone operator
is busy. The hot water
cools down. The zephyr
smells like mint.
A man named Q is
an ex-convict from Kiev.
A fowl dances a jig.

4.
Juliette's final kiss.
It's going to be night.
The dawn gives me head.
Quick, give me the borscht.
The plums tasted good.
I ate 26 of them:
the last three I call XYZ.

PSYCHOLOGICAL NOVEL

Just as Gulliver
I have traveled, have sold
my car stuffed with pillows,
have taken a basketball
and slam-dunked it
into a dry mouth; and now
only bad salad dressing will be persecuted.

All the signs reported themselves silently as if
there were no motives to offer.
I was supposed to read each one carefully
and pick out the agents and voodoo.
If another piece of fucking plastic
is found in my food
I may become a secessionist.

We're dealing with troubled waters and antiques
in our middle years.
As a child I wanted so
to smash cymbals and bottles.
I am like Charles Dickens.
I have read Thackeray and Trollope:
my taste has latitude
as well as darkness
in the sense of a vague forest
that I wander through, later finding
out that it was all a series of stage props.
And I have forgotten my lines
being the understudy.

There was some Frenchie who
wrote so well about
the Russia he never had been to.
Some characters are mentioned
who suffer no guilt.

In any house or apartment
the furniture is an important asset.

Going nowhere
is the scenic route.

Feel what you may.
Hopefully no sentimentalism
will keep you from enjoying
what there is to enjoy.

All your old coins and stamps.
Description upon description.
Keep an eye on the furniture.
It may replace the library.

"QUICKLY HE THE X…"

Quickly he the X
and she the Y
and the but the and the not
the X the Y
a and but nor neither XY.

She he the nothing but the I.

Nowhere not yet,
A nor B nor X nor Y.
She not yet.
He already a lot.
She not not never.
He too soon, all, all.

Gently, he she again,
rapidly, rapidly, rapidly.

She yes more more,
he rigidly I.
Yes, she, and yes, he,
together, both.

RUPTURE

1. Caged Streams

We, our whalers, on its back, catch shiver. Our gales,
delirious, went blind, blues; this morning it rained. Piazza roll
variations of snow, revealing all with Giacometti, the paving
coins, lucky dolls, piazza variations of snow. Forget it, the
way running gently of laughter. Of passage slings.
Continuing bed, gardens, bat-like once with eloquence. The
eyes bled. Mulch. Iowa deem Hog-tie clubs, down seed, half
in station slips, wipe fireworks, disease or plague. Domicile,
best borne.

2. Who's House?

His house is forgotten noise. My house is his house. Infinite
possibilities. The blue river running beneath the house. We
swim. I swim. He swims. All the tenses. The Indians live
there. We are the Indians. I am a red Indian. He is also. We
are joking entirely. We lie to ourselves everyday, and only we
believe our fantasies anymore. He is a bum who sleeps in
Astor Place subway station. Me too. His face is red from
drinking, drinking red wine. That is the only river. People
pass by. People pity us. I am not an Indian. What am I doing
in New York City? His house is not really my house. I lied. I
lied. I lied. Do you feel any better? I do.

3. Square Box

Fucking fright, forget caresses. Miscreants onrushing, ancient
moors. Tadpoles for cash: the solitary reproach. Phrasing
usefulness: "boat of his forgetfulness." Hint of woman,
other ears. Oblong by it, therefore harmful. People do not
refuse. To be a germ, pistils and poking. The percolator
exercise for God's sake. In American specimens, basement
law is appreciated. Box, cigarettes, honey? Climax gardens,
his fancy. Play in the refrigerator: quite breathless.

THE FIELD GOAL UNIT

In the meeting room, very immense and without end, I meet the poet Charles Olson. We are waiting around for our monthly unemployment checks. He tells me that he thought the Cowboys had a good chance this year to win. The debris, or the pieces, or the flecks, or the gestalt, or the flecks, or the pieces, or the....

I see the field goal unit marching on to the field. The opposing general is taking a shit. Let's take advantage of him while he has his pants down. A quick snap, the hold is good, and the kick. The ball is tumbling, tumbling like a spark, like an ember. I think it looks more like the challenger shuttle launch. The whole point of life, to the field goal unit, is to pierce the uprights.

I then wondered why a fight didn't break out in this room. I thought that I was somewhere action-packed. Once, many years ago, I caught an uppercut at a punk rock gig. Blackout.

I go to my high school reunion and I see all these old people with tired worn out looks, and I immediately get bored and go outside the Hyatt Regency and I have a drink at the closest bar. It is snowing and why is it snowing? At the bar I drink a scotch and ginger ale. I become warm. I step outside for a minute to get some fresh air. I cannot believe that my best friend from high school is now a preacher and a religious fanatic. What the fuck happened? I see a cop car driving slow, down the street, out of the corner of my eye. Suddenly I see the ghost of Thomas Pynchon who has been dead for years. His face is unshaven, and he's wearing a leather hat. I see him sitting at his desk. He is writing the next Paterson perhaps. He pauses for a minute, in a dramatic painful creative indecision, in search of "le mot juste." I pack a snowball at his silent beckoning. I see the face of Pynchon, or was his name Tom Storm? I recreate. I pack an extra-big hard snowball. I see the cop car coming closer to me, and the driver's side window is open exposing a suntanned mustached officer of the law. I see the evil smile of

Pynchon. He speaks. He says "after Modernism, what?" I see his thin hand fondling a rare first edition copy of 3 Lives by Gertrude Stein. I throw the snowball and it hits the police officer in the face. The car stops. Red, red, and red! I head back towards the bar, quickly.

In a few moments, I feel a hand on my shoulder, and I see this cop wiggle his finger like this. And he says "let's go."

I am interrogated at the station. I am made to feel like I am going through a mock execution. What's your name? Is that your name? Do you know this guy? Let's see your tax returns! A private investigator walks in the room, punches me a few times, and he asks me a few questions like "so, you know this guy, Bobby Fischer?"

"Never heard of him...."

"You lie!" I get punched again. They have photographs. I get thrown into a cell with a guy who looks like a fucked-up version of Terence McKenna. I am bleeding. I sleep and have a nightmare about a snowman made by children which resembles Gertrude Stein. In the morning, light years away, they let me go. They tell me "sorry, you're the wrong guy..."

It's morning and the acrid sky is blue and painful. Or as the poet Charles Olson once told me in another caustic dream: "the sky is so poignant/poignant to the point/of pain/and the sun/is a lawyer's argument/as sharp as infinity."

THE IMPORTANCE OF BEING ERNEST BORGNINE

January 24, 1917 it begins virtuous. He has a bad day at black rock. Parents of the law out of the labyrinth of the forest. He dies within the fiery walls of The Poseidon. He dies for a fervid love. He can't live without her. Without Ernest, the body transforms into a morass of debris, toxic commodities unrelated to meaning. Here, take it. Grasp it. This is the tactile future, and virtual transgression cleans all.

Travel to the end, journey to the center of the earth. Ernest is the pilgrimage's limit or its sex, the second fiddle to whoever has the war face, the basement jaunt of the world. "You may know where dreams come true...." His new movie. And "new" movie means everything. I was the cowboy who marched on the red plains of Tunisia. I am the cop who hijacked a rebel satellite.

New York City is my prison and I'm its cab driver. He lived in Milan. But no one who drives a cab is from America. An over-achiever. A cowboy of capitalism. Squarish patterns of grimy plaster, pitted opening / chess moves. The way for a true homosexuality next to the fake ones depicted on Channel 11. The noon bell rings repeatedly. And there are beautiful boys in the alley sucking each other. They eat and drink, swallow and Ernest is in leather. It's late, after the depraved clubs have closed. No one pays any attention to them. They exist in that space in skull I call "nowhere's ville."

Beautiful eyes are filled with tears. Ernest lowers his head into that quagmire of sores and latent tendencies. He's on equity wage, he has a family. News has come of his father's death, crucified in the mountains of Albania. He is erect and feels the rise of testosterone on the planet. Distended endings. Advertisement of addiction.

The opaque surfaces of Ernest's cheeks. The billboard goes up, a new movie, a way of thinking is arranged. I said a "new" movie! Let's fight this war, and let's get laid. We have our ugly wives, army groupies, and young boys who love to fuck. Short, twisting, aggressively, between two alleys, the sight of the boy's face.

THE LIFE AND TIMES OF GENESIS P-ORRIDGE

When the cold warriors quit where are all the ideas for democracy? Saving Venice is what we're all about. Vanessa was this beautiful black girl and she would come having walked in the waters of that certainty. Very friendly. I can't take the train, there's a strike at the station. Another new abuse, avenged by the abuser himself. I liked the corpse, it looked like a roast all trussed up with a string. A lot of sweat at least. Everything returns to normal. The great imitation. I dream that those vultures were coming back. It was an exciting dream. Eastern Europe on the line. People committed to helping you achieve your long-term objectives. The third man who comes through that door.... Hairs mixing with hairs and here, go over this threshold with me. I want someone who'll support me. Sex is public, you thought your five-year plans were dead? If there's no time, then it must be drifting. The woman isn't dead, but jealousy is alive. Myra Hindley is very friendly. He brought his anguish. I want an all-out picnic. Futures and swaps. We forget the streams that come from nowhere. I know criminals. I have loved some of them. But who am I?

All in humanity's pile, lying on top of
one another, sweating paganism
"thanks for moving over buddy"
Sperm in the mail, fax it instead
magically crazily all at once
tattooed firm footing in reference
alphabet soup, in summit
in bowls of yesteryear
sometimes words emerge from boiling
pierced dickhead -- no other way
I am the other, shoe-polish's destiny
orchestra's sun-suit

"Let's play I'll be fiction and you be the face of
another world. Let's play you be fiction and I'll be
the face of another will."
                                        -- Norma Cole

THESE MOMENTS WHICH WE CANNOT KEEP

I've just checked the resources, the ever-filled
glass of your wine that I always keep,
but then my mother returns from her visit
to the rose garden slightly bewildered;
and I hide the glass because it seems that
I'm always drinking in front of her.
What about that friend who I never see,
who claims to be in some theater production
on the other side of town, and who is crazy
from time to time? Where is she?
And then it rains, and I sit on the roof
and bring a folding chair thinking of you and
certain parts of Asia. In the country
there, it is so nice that I want to return.
I spent my entire childhood on a rope swing
suspended from a tree; I think that my father
built it, but it could have been my uncle
who still claims he's from Portugal.
Once, he tried to rebuild a Model A,
after being influenced by some movie he saw.
That car is still in the backyard,
some house in Northern California, my grandfather's.
My family is so far away now, that in
their absence, I start to do my impressions of them,
which are never really hard to do.
I agree, it gets to be lonely at certain hours
late on Sunday.
Sometimes, I just want to embrace anyone,
wherever, and tell them that it's better
to be alive than dead.
Sometimes, I just want to talk to someone all night.
Can you believe it when you're broke,
and I used to have so much money: where did it all go?
I don't think about money unless I have none.
I still enjoy those things which I can never buy,
and things that I already have. Things that are free
are the most valuable to me, they are rare sometimes.
To go outside, and to run into friends on the street

sometimes, to feel the wind in your face and the night
all over the sky; nothing's better.
To stop by the store, or the bakery which comes
alive around midnight, when they bake the bread,
and to pick up a hot loaf for a dollar.
And then, coming home, eating it and rereading
a letter which arrived yesterday, quite by surprise.
Just thinking about how some of the evening's plans
that were called off, and not worrying about it.
It OK to stay home and be with yourself.
I remember those days of failure, other times
of indecision, some bewilderment, but I was
always somehow able to bounce back from
those depths, and the first morning afterwards
was not that bad.
I always love the same things
like the blue of the sky.
I liked parks and wide open spaces.
I always liked to look out over the bay, and watch
the wind move the waters
to wilder shores of love.
The clouds, my father with me, the city scenes.
I came here to end something, something
that would not end by itself, by sticking it out,
and let time pass in its forgetting,
but I also came here to begin something else.
I do not know what exactly, maybe more failures,
indecision, and bewilderment, the same foolish things.
Maybe some good that I cannot imagine just yet.
But above all, to live and to be free.
What was I thinking all this time?
Was my general outlook the same?
I still do not know why Nancy called me
late in the night, I haven't talked to her in a month.
I don't know why I haven't called her earlier.
We all get caught up in other things and people.
I try to convince myself that it could be no other way.
Night is so unique the way it is, why change it?

I worry too much about the wrong things,
especially if I have the time to worry.
I agree that life can be miserable,
but to make something out of life that
was never there means a great deal to me.
The mysteries of life will always fascinate me.
I hear so many conversations around this city,
some that I want to join, others I want to exit.
Most of our friends have arguments that are the same
arguments.
I try to argue less and less.
When Nancy came, we sat down and drank coffee,
and we talked about what we did last night.
Later, we went to Washington Square Park
and sat down in the sun, drank some wine
with her thoughts of Italy.
I thought of myself drowning in someone else's
library for a few hours and finding books I'd never heard of.
I'd very much like to live my life here in the stacks
of The San Francisco Public Library,
or near the shelves of some bookcase.
But, the last time it rained, I caught cold.
I imagine that it won't rain for quite a while
since it's coming close to the summer.
We've had so many conversations about the seasons,
which ones we liked the most.
I remember the sound of last night
when the music ended,
some boat in the bay, off North Beach.
A horn that would sound off
every minute "Ooo-ahh!"
And it went on all night.
When I was younger,
I used to watch the red lights
on top of Twin Peaks.
Now the music of the bar
stops around one-thirty
in the morning and I'm usually awake.
And by two, the streets are quiet.
It's a gray night.

Melancholy is the spirit
of our streets
and there's no doubting it.
I love this city
when it's like this,
so sad.

"THIS IS A CHUNK…"

This is a chunk of writing that is missing a quality. Can you find what's missing? Possibly you can, just try. I'll wait for you to find it and ask you again at dusk as soon as I finish. A wind blows through this door by a girl with curious hands. Right, it's night. Any color? You know that! I walk down a path in a park, and I say to a city:

"Within a story, a group of birds fly upward."

I'm a son of a railroad man. My mother stays in a villa in California, but south of San Francisco by six hours driving. I stay at a flat at Folsom and Ninth, by Limbo and Slim's. Good things about today: cash, food, pussy, and colorful talk.

Find your path in this park. Lost, you turn around. Go away, but you can't! A trip that will go on without you, and you still can't find mama: you can't find it. On a bus. Lost in a ghastly milky flow, as smooth as pajamas, silk as if hair. Your hairshirt is what you want. And want is all about us. Say your story, paint it into a living form. Possibly I'm as lost as you look, sound from visuals. Stop, start. It's all Norma's fault.

up information as it was now
if you got music wrong you got sick
a child dashing a baby on its back
spiral's social, slight's out
unit's turn, opinion's portals
mountain's staying, shadow's authority

I'm in the living room of my mom's condo. I'm watching TV and I'm watching you. A program about you is on right now. It's fascinating. I sip my calistoga and light a cigar. I fought with a girl today, and now I study philosophy. Marx and things similar. All unpopular in your mind. I want to study a philosophy, not Marx, or Plato, but I can't. I can't say who.

Find out what's missing? I would say if I could. Twilight's curtain. Good luck, and now I find my room, my cot, in Chinatown. You can go away too. It's your choosing. Night has a last word.

TWILIGHT

I'm twenty-eight now, unmarried,
        and you're twenty-nine. The noise of the birds.
I cannot see what's happening up there, in this purple
        morning, but the beats of white wings
converse with our prolonged conversation about the nature
        of all things going their separate ways.

"Tell me a story" someone said wearing a baseball cap.
        We journeyed and were never lost in those few
moments on bristling grass, although where were we?
        To the right, the marriage of sky and water.
Somewhere out there are the seven islands, now replaced
        by seven imperceptible hills that only whistle.

Who wrote the book entitled I Hang Around With Silence
        At Santa Cruz? At night, sometimes, I fall and fall
to the depths, but it's only a prank, see?
        Who can sleep with that fucking racket? Sorry,
the door has been left unhinged by an annoying roommate.

I'll sing to the several futures of America of baseball daily
        in Siberia and Yugoslavia, when writing this I used
both sides of the mirror so everyone could read it. You take
        a paintbrush and make swirls in blue and black
and call it a love song. When the paint dries I move my hand
        over the surface and read like the blind do.

As I live, you press me
        to forge more hymns to the night,
but we do not use gasoline, even though it's love.
        Whose skin requires policing
when the love letters discontinue?
        I thought that they were dead flowers, but
perhaps they were corpses acting beautiful. I took
        a poll of your solitudes, and plucked
a few notes on the harpsichord and we were
        all beguiled by the melancholy.

My vision is of nothing but waves
        expiring peacefully beneath the cliffs.
A flutist off in the distance playing some Bach,
        walking back and forth. This man may keep
the truth from us. The truth about what happened.
        Walter, the pollen, cobra, who?

The fire sang this as the night came.
        Do not look at me, because I didn't say it.
The flowers spoke to you in whispers, and you
        looked painfully concerned:
"Love us for what we are, not for what we are not,
        not for what we may be." They had
children's voices and wore children's clothes.

I then abandoned Christ's ego
        for better flavors of ice cream,
and many different styles of pancakes.
        You say "your eyes, your eyebrows...."
I throw up a tent and secretly believe that
        my home is on the 13th floor of some
building in the Western Addition.

Someday, madmen will shoot guns at the orange trains.
        Someday, someone will run me over with his car,
because he took the scenic view. Unbelievably interesting.

Then, I compare myself to Audrey Hepburn,
        with irony, was she not a cunning stunt?
Audrey! We should have children, and name them
        after Greek gods and goddesses.

If you leave me soon, I ask you now:
        "where shall we meet again?"
On a riverboat? In some primitive tribe?
        On a bus near the corner of 16th and Mission?
The hours speak of hurricanes and seduction.
        When I first came here, this city was so fast,
I couldn't possibly take everything in. No one will
        ever penetrate the secrets of the box.

But the mind is a whore, sometimes never feeling
        shame when all naked for all to see.
Unraveling and unraveling, is there any more fabric?
        Always when I reach for you, Audrey,
you are not there, and I cannot see anything.
        The light has expired, the hills are barren.
Aging hands write me a postcard once
        in a while, signed Lady Hepburn.

If not for those self-evident truths,
        something else violent and stronger will
cause my heart to burst. An implosion....
        An intense fire which sometimes makes me
cowardly. Sometimes, I cannot talk about it
        because it is too miserable.
Those words would be a golden chalice
        which contains each one of my pains.
I speak, and speak, and speak of pain and world
        you don't listen. The world knows nothing
of human pain, and it cannot comprehend misery.
        It is dull and without spirit.

To withdraw from the world for a minute and to think:
        that will prove that I am not a beast.
And I defend myself from the chaos.
        But maybe, there are no more songs to sing,
no more homages to the past. If we don't know the past,
        we are dead, as dead as the world.

One day you will love me without me.
        One day you will get off.
One day neither one of us will be able to get it up.
        One day poetry will eat itself.
One day poetry will choke on its own vomit.

The night becomes more ferocious, and sex
         becomes a temporary stay from misery.
Too many hustlers in every city, even San
         Francisco, tempting you, soliciting you....
Some songs too, have become advertisements,
         and like religion, it has nothing to offer my spirit.
Too addictive, and without beauty.

I am guilty of love, and of anarchy.
         I have lived a mundane life, but
one or twice I saw the pure white light.
         Poetry. I came from you, and
I will return to you. Between the moment
         when a flower is plucked and when it is
given, lies an eternity. But I am only eternal
         in sleep and in the darkest shadows.

I have always recognized the quick speed
         of life, moments pass, and loves pass.
Death will only be paid to me by living intensely.
         I try to rid myself of all illusions,
but truth is difficult to live with.
         I look for an inner vision, and then
an aurora appears briefly, a golden glow in the night.
         I do not know who to tell....
The light of myself is from myself and cannot
         be spoken.

Poets will go to hell
         and beauty will be punished.
Athlete of the world,
         and biographer, tell me when
you have tamed those living terrors.
         Come to me
someday, when you have seen
         something else other than yourself.
Sing to me when your vanity
         has subsided.

Hang it all. Let me see the light,
          the tortured self, the human death,
or let me read the tortured word.
          We have all put on masks,
and when taken slowly
          off like skin, reveal death.

V (VERBS, HOW TO USE THEM)

1.

Your long absence pigments the canvas of my brutal life, my face gnarls still today as when I had fornicated with you, but in pain. Never do I condescend to your silence, but blur the void with my feeble paint brush, on my painting, without talent, but which nonetheless embodies our short-lived yet intense fiery love. Today I plunge beneath the surface of appearances and half-truths, and infect myself with lame nostalgia for the naivete of youth and simpleness. Your face, your body, your voice, everything muddles with time and Tom Collins. Childhood and romantic memories jostle with fiction as I, a faithful servant to the believable and strong images, try to write our unknown history, unknown to the media. This problem, or dilemma, or whatever-the-fuck, never reconciles with the past. I whisper, not to you or your memory, but to truth.

2.

Richard Brautigan gnarls before his assassin, a CIA agent. Thus the real story (KPFA) blurs and plunges into the predictable throes of a writer, a suicide. Fact jostles with fiction, Brautigan, author of the ignored book "Rommel Drives Deep Into The Desert," a political target. It has been whispered to me that Brautigan fornicated with many women, their faces and bodies on covers of his books, embodied the fact of their lovemaking. Why his books are muddled with subversive codes has never been reconciled with his life and supposed suicide. Death pigments our image of "that dirty hippy" Brautigan, but we have not yet condescended to the possibility of his murder in a cabin in Northern California. Brautigan's main interests: fishing, fighting. and fucking. The CIA tried to infect Brautigan with cancer, but he still wrote a few more novels, influential, and hero to the young.

3.

I embody the sitcom of your newscast, and yellow trucks condescend to pedestrians in every American city. The dog gnarls, infected with rabies, not biting today. But hurt, I reconcile the matter with the dog's owner, Bucky Dent, ex-Yankee shortstop. Washington Square Park jostles with the wind of Tompkins Square Park in my mind. A whisper that whispers itself to me "Ida Lupino, red dress, murder." I write the words down as a detective. My leading lady muddles her words, as I plunge a knife into the victim (Oh no! a borrowed scene from a Robbe-Grillet novel). This story blurs with another story about a young girl named Jennifer. She refuses to fornicate with me, a real frigid high school type, "Oh no!" My manhood is not going to pigment your womanhood, what little there, in that girlhood, tonight.

WHAT IS KNOWN AND HOW YOU ARRIVED
THERE SAFELY

She was silent
when the princely gods asked
her for advice.
The toxic chemicals
invited us
to this gold ball.
We arrived unannounced.
We were not there.
She gave him blindness.

When they asked.
A few pills, a few
beauty secrets away
from Bermuda.
Your promises to frogs.
Sadness, melancholy.
"Image and metaphor
are no use to me" he said.
He flew away with a series of ducks;
south for the winter.
He studied, and he studied, and he
telegraphed his secret knowledge to me.

Instead of the profound
wisdom of the Analects
he would send me an issue
of The New York Times
and a comic book entitled "Yummy Fur."
Now we live in a desert.
No lamenting will solve the riddle,
but we can still pretend
that we understand;
and suddenly we were on a stage.
Now it is too fast, you think,
and can we stop?
How did you get so knowledgeable?

I met her again and told her the brief story.
She said: "I think they are a distant relative."
You told me "I am Chinese" and "not Japanese."
I was impressed by her conversion
to Lesbianism,
and now she does not love me anymore.

I wrote to her,
one hand toward the ground,
one toward the sun.
Sadness and melancholy.
The Indians will disappear, I think.
I did not want
to return to childhood,
but just wanted the confusion.

William Carlos Williams
never meant anything
except to the military:
he wrote in a secret code
to the enemy
whoever the enemy is this month.

The Apache, the Navajo, the Polish.
Shall we agree on the Polish?
"I declare war on Poland!"
Their army represented
very well
in an Alfred Jarry play.
There are no more Indians.
This is about sadness
and melancholy.

YELLOW YELLOW YELLOW

Speak English to me.
This is a love song ....
How did you know?
I will say I love only if it has never been said before.

When I say "unknown pleasures."
I say it exactly as it has been written years ago, by who?
By Marcel Proust in Remembrance of Things Past.
I read that book like a sheriff who is searching for a old
peanut.
Or just the smell of one.
Or a policeman looking for one-liners
always thinking of someone named Cassavetes.
Or was it Casanova?

The sheets are stained with the color of love
and we are painters by trade.
I feel sorry for you when you have to define you
or when you have to define the blue world
with the idiotic gaze of one looking at the sky
while drinking in a boat.
I once saw a poet drinking orange juice
in a worsening situation.
And now, I am always some character
eternally ascending a staircase in the mind
of a poet, in a dream possibly,
reading a newspaper, the headline reads "Rocky Turns
Yellow,"
with someone who is not my wife, nor named Sheila.

But you are yellow y-clept yellow.
You say you love me after much rehearsal.
You had quite a lot of practice in your formative years
because you were a method actor,
and now, your love is a ripe orange.

But never mind that your oranges
are really lemons, like Frederico.

I will say that I love you and you
will swoon dramatically and say what it
is like to feel like a woman
and it will seem to you also as if
no one had ever used these words
in a novel or a poem
or a treatise on the human emotions,
or in any sentence ever uttered by an utterer,
and I was the first.

Maybe.
Yellow?
Yellow!

Z (TO BE SPOKEN IN A WHISPER)

Texaco night sticky struck
always you pull
coyly exploded secrecy
curled hair, bedwetter's lover
tossed creature pissing
old free zones
understanding the signatures
voodoo's bellydance, smile's boot
piano crept like a needle
a swirl of torture
the crabgrass pops
sold no freeze
tunneling kisses to follow
sucking pomegranate
warm files of S. A. (buzz)
dizzying port, foreign scent (buzz)
unraveling fingers in the dark (buzz, buzz)
speed will scatter pearls (buzz, buzz)

move into one solid line, lights glare
single file, automobile's slavery
caution ahead, poets at work
the knives are dull today, aren't they?
who invented porridge?
always you pull, buzz
I am everything on your special list
I'm waiting too, bang
and it's you, bang-bang
the telephone rang, my turn
I feel your fangs, blood
we are house of paper
always you pull
bloody buzzing

moistness first, grinding worse
silkworms move her own hex
I have my own hex, in my tuckerbag
and it's working, mixing the anagrams
head in soup, pepper to bend
spinning hearts swing her something
wheel's flirtation rammed the warning
insects around love's firelight
zen door feels
revenge soup
I kissed warm files
in the form of an infection
stubborn magnets kick the trash
licked cleaned by mister tuckerbug
always you pull
S. A. (knock knock)
who's that?
buzz
ear candy, buzz
how do you like the buzzing
in your holes, buzz?
Am I able to do it?
able to give Andrea an apple
His name was Abel
and I'm Zed, how do you do?
in the giant art deco bed
we open this book
together, with four hands
and read about Eve and Adam

find the last grid pattern
the city lies before you
rearrange and transform
the letters go back and forth
from A to Z

Book Six: Welcome To The Cabaret (1992)

STRANGERS MEETING THE COURSE IN
PAINTED VOICE

what is this?
what collision?
and I read that brutal accusation
of tearing and laughed red
this is about the length of a circle
and the seepage comes through
how do you look at it?

I can say what I want
no reply to the other's silence
how it is to dance, being misunderstood
that's not a problem
of the many circuses of voices
of amusement parks and words
of this first collision
it's possible that I go away just now
meteor: she is in another country
the inventory temple: volume of birds
I don't know which one
blow: the impact of noise

meeting cool's limit, that you're very young
all these explanations about the reasons
reasons and solutions and excuses about us
some of the things that I have to endure
waking up in the midst of the course
the hullabaloo of science and punishment
using the propositions I learned
I ask of you: fold calm paper
suffer the depression of the mind eating itself
by road or plane, fatigue and partial nudity

am I like you?
painted chance roll
by load or plague
seepage of words comes through
a correction of shapes used
the blow returns

am I like those?
fly like a bird
needleboats floating in San Sabba
swimming in bitches' brew
the reader finds their suicide
fold the road, move its parts
how do you look?

I have to endure, face
the fist of history
come home, and apply the coat to the exterior
and come to me
stranger, strange as a new lover
or a new plant which causes such strange things
by line or boat
I am here now

OBVIOUS TARGETS

I'm going to tell you a story first, and then
read someone else's story. Life becomes most
exciting when you continue in this way.
I forgot what I told you before, and the time before
that, but that is still true today, although it may be dated.

The hunters come up to our doorstep every day.
I'm getting tired of saying "no, thank you."
I better put a sign out there saying "No Soliciting."
But it's a party here, almost every day, and it may
be that were all here together for a reason.
Maybe not. I'll be so unhappy to go, knowing
no other life apart from life listening to this jukebox.

My anger has no person to go with it anymore.
So that causes me to be more experimental in my hates.
Maybe, knowing that tonight we will
be trying a different dish is enough.

Throwing rocks at bottles may be too entertaining
for children, but not for me. I listen to the crack and
bing of life, and it makes me happy knowing
that it's not my bones, but something else that's breaking,
man-made and inert.

Let me interrupt to say
that in looking back on these past seasons
that I am still capable of love.
And I am the arrow going towards you the place.

THE SINGER

He flatly denies any intimate involvement
with the other obscure French poet
while witnessed by gossiping birds
but in the blue light the singer
is trapped in his cage as well, repeating songs of love
with artful indifference towards the audience
you don't know if he means it
or which mechanical stars are baboons despite ourselves
with old contiguity, separateness
amplified by rescued fugues

the singer's frozen dreams
come from the blue sandwich world
beyond good and Elvis
or an impersonator with a loss of hair
shoe polish jazz beckons yet another martini
already in my swollen mouth a labyrinth
are you willing to enter the dragon?

a woman wears a long dress, her sepia tones are exquisite
her shoulder's shadows call to the lens of the lover
focus in on the nape of the song
tarantella, fall into you and collapse
piano player's hands trespass over
the mason-dixon line and suggest love's war
an ensemble of our dreams nightmares
a flower emerges from his buttonhole
her fruity lips are red, a parody of red
the singer's eyelids hold back fake tears
but we are real would-be lovers
and the velvet song is the background hum

THE WRONG NAME

in this massive transposed city mum-mouthed
pierce me dazzle, razzamatazz puzzle
pierce me city of invented hope
heavy-lagging fog
(weighty lips that go slow, swarthy)
a hook of my insides crush
wanting that mouth and that face
snow on its lips
malted air, mouth's smithy

your eyes are beerbrown, babe
(reminding you of rivershore's junk)
rouse motherlove, incite dwarfqueen
to the hologram zoo its dubious barkers
lost in voice's spiderweb, stuck
my dreams are fat, blue, and greedy
wishes that unweave aren't true
the slot of want

my liquorking falling in bachelor's oil
like a gravedigger slips into a grave
and speaks with Yorick
watery drinks collect at her acquiescent ginpit
and turn on the jittery heartstrings
spilled beer on my smokesuit
but reincarnation is a new idea

you counterfeit goat, I'm lapping up
your mellifluous buttersea
listen to mattress tapping, saying again "thud"
and her legs, yes rubbing "plop"

I blame me, not William
I blame the horns of opprobrium
and the meatsmelling vampire
delving for liable ants and oil too
with his imperious fangs, his drill bits
how far can this go? hit anything yet?
turn around black, turn ice cream cone
yearning for purity
fade to black

SICK MOON
(for Victoria Straub)

all beauty exists for this simple reason
   once claiming to be humane sparkle clear
but is exactly opposite, not a mirror, nor a reason
   barking up your treetrunk, reformed
entering your squalid room leaving its marks
   burning vision which awakens demon in your soul
pressing on your pink earlobes without impunity
   enjoyable?

   simultaneously my mind is and is not
fixed on the corpses that I have witnessed / repetition
   murders were unexplained, unthinkable
bodies ripped open by excess of love
   and then, their unbearable stench looks up
where no beautiful thing exists at all / accursed share
   looking for somewhere to pilfer, or exploit
and there, over there, and the other place
   this manual, auto-pilot, instructions for use

"didn't think of looking there" sings Petrarch
   over there, a blob of white balanced
mush in the sky, which looks unmistakably like
   an eye which has been severed
split through middle with divine fever (barbarous)

   where pale moon was (leaves scene)
in place of moon (no one can touch this sickness)
   this distorted face is as temporary as myself
no one can remember this mask (murderer) with time

REVEILLE

wake up and drive the cab
have at least one fulgurating thought
my ship lost at sea with speed
wearing a black beret
horn with a different sound
warning call, rushing too fast
let's do some blow

blow up and wear this song
buy at least one horn
my ship crashes into forgotten island
driving black car
thought with a different sound
desolate sand and solitude
let's wake up the red girl

welcome to my reliant cities
welcome to the assured heart of the fix
welcome boys and girls
the shipwreck of my voice

no primal scenes
island of the dead
a labyrinth
secrets under silence
shattered mind
broken meanings
you trust me
I trust you

CAR COMING

Soon, it will suddenly end, and night
will wrap around us like a cold blanket
while trumpets play their final notes.
Oddly enough, your face is fading and
returning in my mind, in your absence.

Some day, the big car will come,
the wave will crush us,
but we'll be safe if we have
a green surfboard by the bed.
I say this because it was your dream.
The car will come any moment, any hour,
and we must be ready to jump in.

The water may be cold at first.
You just don't know till you touch.
And we will need someone to drive that car.
Can you drive a stick shift?
Jesus will come one day,
but he only has a mule with room for two.
My cadillac has room for ten.
Are you ready to go for a ride?
I have no idea where we're going.

Just drop what you have in your hands.
The lights are blinking.

HOTEL UNIVERSE

it was before becoming the universe
upsetting the time, it was not the universe at all
but just "an in-between" of settings, of moods
and it said something about my homosexuality
before my prison, I had to pay to stay here

all the images were redefined, and touched up
my hands were also touching her shoulders
her body was not a universal body
wearing a gown of ten year's amnesia
she should be virginal and pure, as I forget her

there's more traffic of people checking
in and out of here than on the freeway
but why should I think about this?
why should I rent a room in this body?
her voice was like honey, I felt it down
to my bones, and my brittle bones said
"tenderness, tenderness"

my house is not like any old house
it's a rusty old can in the gutter
but look at me in a moment of sobriety
whipped in humanity's humility
we all stay at this hotel for only so long
then time's up, move your shit, scotoma!
the universal / its constant turning into the other / or itself
how far from me it is, from this understanding
voices in the hallway carrying a pipe
in this dirty old hotel on a lonely planet
that doesn't play my dilapidated records anymore

EROS

tactile portrait of the family
        it's us, rose "that's an order"

not born of the ocean, strongly said /
what to do about the girl?
our fabric, greasy of /
and for skin: "not a problem for me"
prodigy of Mercury, the course for girls /
with speed

finaglers of the sun have turned cruel like buttermilk
the assault of names, forgotten glasses   think!
mouth of you /
sees the old lexicon and reads

in plain brilliance of a frozen kiss /
novel /
photograph
under laughter: a bitter soup with a charge of words
silence takes a blank swing at space and misses

you, truly the most beautiful shape of water,
couldn't be a Spartan
.....freshly born between acts /
each moment is a level reached
those serpents have died where no one is /
but servants

allow me to be on the table /
to open the session /
the board meeting begins
we listen   (mystery: sex organs) yet that noise
thunders repeatedly
childhood: the source of which /
my parent's bed

with the unheard sound /
or your orifices /
behind the keyhole lies MAMA
if you have /
spare change /
sexual endurance /
or the staying power
of figuring out a phallic enigma, go look

UNDERNEATH SKIN

her temples anointed
with plausibility
get out of this skin
or go over this untried peak
bathing in moonlight
simple as that night which
hemorrhages into sun
pain is the answer
youth does not solve
mortality of the mask
our age is a consumed one
interrupted by a liberating love
death also peeling with impunity
like a snake in the desert
we connect and wrap our bodies
we steal its brief signs
and take in history
"what is beauty?" she asks
blowing its own horn

IN THE DRAMA/NOT OUT

watch out roots, my torn hair
        you were hoodwinked easy, weren't you?
while participating in a lazy job or strict organization
        you were the force that through you
I exist as the yellow choice of abandonment
        yet with sempiternal time, I may become involved
with the practice of pitting reversals / obverse of its image
        in circles where violence is more shy & hidden

off with my shoes, I'm home the repetition of twilight
        the sun ricocheting off the broken marble & pieces
a woman's temper is never easy to deal with
        ensued violence where slapping is a revenge of hand
was trapped and prepared like dinner
        mental strength that pits and sings, and subtends
the intricacies of the invented, supports the latticework

                yes, you do not know, feel, apart
                or together, from anything's other, or
                the other's other, yes, you do not feel
                let's be in between, in unison, colored
                between the contiguous monotony
                that happens weekly, connected to habit
                let my body be used for bait, the refractory
                at their will, the old fishermen, can I exist
                this, you should do too, I suggest to you
                need me, need this, please my unhappy leaf
                conversing in the darkroom,
                photosynthesis parodying
                this real bond with the exception
                of being out, not in, of the frame

MAXIMUM ROOM CAPACITY

I.

I will excise, curl up like blue flames
take me away from here mister (speaking suitcase)
bought in a store at this price: haggle with a woman
help me now for this once, century 20 expiring
laughing because of / in the face of pain
no room for comfortable thoughts

II.

uncover secret reasons why my good friend Bob
used chainsaw on his girlfriend (not satisfying the never-
ending itch)
he was a good friend other than that

III.

deplete against the distance (curdle)
desperate findings, time to turn in
time to roll over the surface
a shadow in the pool
dripping like pain

IV.

LANDING IN THE MIDDLE OF PAIN:
wall to wall, prevents play
against violent argument
amid copious evidence
all the cards are down
bet it all on my lucky horse

PAINTED STAR

why cry for the dried?
fatal pebble
discover their season
furrowed crime
silent to nails
has left its ears

sign's knives
tears the bullets
coffin bride
a vagabond of words
overwhelming it
reign of dust
eyes cut from meaning
loosens the load
distinguish as blood's hour fades

feathers of heaven
ribbon in sky
buttoned laughter
takes away hot stars
and my one painted face
figurine of my love
will burst
broken apart
unseen by fixed eyelids

ZIP ZIP

olive eyes infrared with tension spirit

definition buries

the secret of the void
fresh corpse's journey towards
attends its funeral: climax of
a surface translation of yellow rain
pre-morning hills sense physical heat

waves are solemn, abstract
feathered with freedom
wet salty stone beckons
milks my mortality

looking at the sky
standing alone, ameliorated
painted yellow
closure by zipper
clouds close discharge
beetles achieve orgasm
by mutual masturbation

"I pose you your question: shall you uncover honey /
where maggots are?" (Charles Olson)

a/ opening of trust

b/ human voice meets bird's voice

invisible copulation

FIRST BREATH, LAST PLACE

first love exists as / ripping of flesh as / a rose
protected in a glass jar / wilting, petals falling one by one
first bamboozle, plastic juggernaut: juggling the jugs?

"Only the real negation of culture can preserve its meaning."

our life composed like a sitcom (trente minutes)
thought of pure white snow (steal -- big fat man: ol(d)son)
ROTATION : EVERY TEN MINUTES

black race, and Hamlet bites
the last hand that breathes (is it possible?)
the sun changes color as we speak
and language can't hold these metaphors
he says "love is as black as anything"
the last letter is more real (first purloined letter)
and has more reality than real estate on a hill

In Braille: THE COMPLETE WORKS OF E. A. POE

   "Reinvent waking up." (Norma Cole)

Ten minutes more of waiting hurts.... /
cleans the skull of its unnecessary debris

we are the brave green men
(intertexual sexual: the poetics of sexuality!)
who exist as your protection
(men who copulate while the book is closed)
the guards of what state?
(let this question ring falsely in your ears)
condoms ruin unknowingly what gods have given to man
(REFERENT: PARADISE) then a new poem
which violently destroys all subjectivity

ERASED:

BLOOD

> When neither eye is open
> And the earth dances.
> Most things happen in twilight
> When the earth dances
> And God is blind as a gigantic bat.
>   -- Jack Spicer

inviolable the square
I once thought, my circular view of history
which regurgitates and palpitates
holding back impetuous blood like a dam
the direction of the mortal arrow
goes that way and grows subtle

her white space yet a distant affair
with blood my face grows stubble
night's infrastructure closes
my eyes half closed (the gloaming)
the other is pounded to slimy oblivion
into your severed house (with sacred books)
brought about by slippery references
and by spurts of blood my pet bat paints,
old cans loaned by whose purblind mother?

she faints the cat prays
on blood's meditation (light tapers....)
not real prayer, entirely unconscious
who's really watching anything but TV?
what choice is there?
to fuck or not to fuck / the eternal....
no real choice, but for the insane
we're the stupid drama
the sacrosanct history of all the earth
yes, look it up (holy man!)
overpowered by the stronger army
blood is a good lubricant

CHAMPS

Fields of lunatics tossing me tips.
They're calling me names. Names that I don't understand.
Words that I don't know. I know most words.
Some foreign language.

Fields of sleeping talking to guess who?
Lunatics dreaming of you, world, calling my name.
Can you hear that brittle emblem?
Her arms are full of roses.

Fields of wondering.
What's my name now? Who are you now?
We're the wandering pair, in this static world.
I'll be the world today.

Fields of killing them now.
They're being pulled out by the roots.
It hurts me more than you.
Let's drive around this curve one more time.

Fields of suspicion in her eyes.
Where's the deck of cards that the palm reader gave you?
She has something, she wants something.
Shake, shake. A snake caressing in her hair.

Fields of more fields.
More "yes." I say "no" to your "no."
I don't want to talk to you right now. Why?
Because I don't want to talk to you right now.

Fields of magic beams.
Check out that new stereo in the car!
The USA of a summer night watching the western stars.
Soon, there will be a gushing flood.

Fields of faces.
In the crowd, somewhere you are standing.
Amid the shadows, and the shopping sprees.
Some ugly faces, old faces, going home, all of them.

Fields of Hamlets.
I wonder who will take your place?
The understudy is somewhere behind the curtain.
The red curtain, the red roses.

Fields of poems and stories.
We are the fiction of this reality.
My story cannot be written.
I die being unable to write it.

Fields of your majesty suppressing our thoughts.
We have a new society yet to form.
New museum yet to erect.
I can't think in this little room.

Fields of genitals in Italian sun.
Flowering in the showers of thinking.
Sweat on the back, burning sensation.
"I" take "you" for "me."

Fields of roses in Northern California.
Silence is what it comes to, Jack!
Going on and on, but stopping once in a while.
Taking in the scenery.

HOODWINKED

sleepwalkers become "they" on the sidewalk
anonymous with their bony masks and little voices
repeating all the dull moments and dirty jokes
you wonder where they all come from, so do I
I grew up in this neighborhood and at no time
more than now have I seen so many eyeless faces
they have become lunatics with protective armour
unremitting are the hustlers in the snare, working it
equally lost and inhuman as tourists, pushing the cart

"you've been had," says the grain in the wood
watch "the fix" drift around the disconsolate street, some are
outside not listening to the beat, tapping on the street
each one's been ripped off in an endless circle
who's really getting the fix and who's not?
all of those silhouettes returning to the dust in the rain
where we came from, returning to unlikely encounters
the dirt and the grime fall away revealing
a luminous point, that is a piece of vital punctuation

a luminous point that was our only moment of real beauty
separated by time punctuated by the canceled life
and your life without motion is overlapping with mine
a point that is the start and the middle and the end
look at that crystal moment, or you'll miss it

DEAD MAN

I smoke from the marvelous mouth
and feel my body trembling with pleasure, alive.
Winds do not scare away the clouds.
Darkness is a powerful liqueur that numbs our senses.
I don't want to be the dead man.

Even if it is cold, I cannot feel it
as a corpse cannot feel the cold ground
he is under. I don't, dead man.

Flowers come and go, music comes from nowhere;
at least a memory of a melody, which pulsates
through my body, not yet dead. I'll check.
Solecisms that pass judgments.

I sit in my country house, the blue lake is nearby,
calm and noiseless. I know the city, and take it with me
to this winter retreat. I have a few bottles of wine.
And sometimes I feel like the dead.
I'm talking to you, dead man.

Grass grows in this rock.
Your face is a blur of lights.
I know that the sun, another face, will come tomorrow.
Bones will not come tomorrow, I'm hoping.
My senses have gone through this phrase, the jump-start of
morning, changing as we do. Dead men never change.
I seek out that eruption.

The earth shakes from time to time
and I have different feelings each time.

A FIRST STEP

shadows tacitly open incipient the window
noiselessly a leaf / sacrifice the alphabet
other lips, plays / inscription residue dwells
strangely you do / reality excerpting guilty

luxurious textures / sound as nothing answered
eject travel awry / number ill beliefs
precipice step of winter / pointed to
assumption of home / or wings journey

a forgetful tinge of wrapped mist

perfect image pitch of birds / foreplay
other steps of desires turn curve
tombs nearly autobiographical step of spring
nearly form an impression / San Francisco

you on videotape / continuance imitates breath
accident announces surprises / burrowing deep, terminated
the bottle broken of past hologram
"imagine favors" / gas, looms untaught leak

SEMPITERNAL ROTATION: MOTION STEPS
OF AUTUMN

imagine end, bending / luggage unprepared literal
always personal touch / twisted, crushed pebbles
yes, brilliant light fulgurating around violence
steps of summer: sun of death

GOTHIC

that music is old and violet outside, it wears on me
devastatingly grey, daily headache nominates the mood
months given out recklessly unfit for spring
golden age full of forgotten tyranny and straight absolutism

"The laws of this sentence, self-proclaimed, but
people read too fast. What happened?"

like you, startled eyes, and teeth (future surgery)
pay homage to a rusty shadow, intimations of black prince
out in legions of an empty desert, void of blue
there is bad blood and no water fondling my senses,
Edward CONTINUITY

soaking morbidity in a tub, light in reflection shines
my green bride was swallowed up by depraved quicksand
my whole life of a rose color though mysterious
yet no one criticizes the Indians when they give out spirit

two white dogs with black spots in a clear bowl
can travel all over the world and multiply with ferocity
my dirge falls into dead glasses until dawn
crank the box yet one more time for Black Peter
(blackmailed?)

I ask you "do you remember the victims, mister?"
mirror that suffers the dark floggings and feminism
poet is no longer a victim like gargoyles
(check "table of contents")
drifts free from the reader's pockets

a machine then perfects the art of subtle plagiarism
the clank of it offers no solace to you or me
(kik clu kik li po kuk sluk)
this is a creaky machine like your body is
do you have Lorenzo's oil in the supply of morgues?

SHOW OF SNOW (ON SECOND AVENUE)

snow struck where always exploded
my lover free zones understand signatures
a thin needle, a swirl torture around unraveling targets
who invented porridge in this house of paper?
always you, bloody moistness first, explaining worse
in my tuckerbag it's baking, mixing cake batter
bread in soup, pepper to grind, love's firelight burns in
supermarkets

always you push me (on the way to Veselka)
how do you like the puzzle?
together, a show with four hands
find the last word which hooks you
city lies before, rearranged transformed
ongoing letters from A to Z
wrong name in massive city (who are you?)
pay me dazzle, razzamatazz jazz amour
pay me city of hope with heavylagging frog of truth
weighty hips go slow walk down St Marks street
a rook of insides move to check weak pieces of life
wanting mouth and face snow on lips
to zoo its bars, I'm lost in voice's prison tres bien ensemble

mine not yours, my king falling in trap like
an olive slipping into waterloo drink
knight to queen's bishop three (what's my name?)
you goat up to buttersea pink floyd
listening to stick tapping, saying again
her peglegs, yes rubbing (alcohol is "the death in life")
I blame me, not welfare, not death camps
I blame horns and Chelsea con men
with their fangs, their snowballs, with their confidences
lose anything yet?

OUROBOROS

Kitchen matches, strike the metal on poverty of the spirit: toast! We're toast in terms of our position in this artist colony. See the masked man: Laszlo Le Fur, the singer in the street. His face is white, his clothes are black…. He's dressed for dinner, but his basking at Powell Street hasn't brought in enough change for a decent dinner at Original Joe's. His bulbous head that people laugh at, they howl: he is the punching bag of our failed poems.

A devil! A microphone in his hand. Where's Tom Jones now? Strike the match and let it bake.

"C'est pire que prévu mais le pire était prévu."

The food for our poor spirits in this solitary place. For the little girl who's nothing but a skeleton now. For the jasmine flowers you've dropped on the way home. By chance, she's the one who's made this miserable world. My old champion was tarred and feathered by living.

The "Little Match Girl" fades before the nuclear light…. The focus is frantic. No more socialist dinner parties to discuss revenge and Leninism. Snake in synthesis.

This fucking world took away my crutch that was a bottle of Jack Daniels, green label. I am big, and I need a big name and a big house. My teeth dig into a steak, a substitution for your neck. Unfocused quicksand is what you are. The words "crazy deep sea diver" are written on my forehead. Your hair is all wet, and I part the curtains. Green and orange, blue and greenblue. Hey, you're a mermaid, of a fishwife. You want a ride in my car? I just bought a Cadillac. A red light obstructs my real designs on you. But hell, I've run red lights before. I go through the door, the window or door (who knows?) and a cop is chasing me, it's my ex-wife! I lose her and fall through the lines on your hand that says "long life, love, and travel" like mine.

THE BLACK PRINCE OF NESTOR BURMA

it's the blatant tarantella, on the map you noodlehead
can't you see that by his black suit he adorns?
ideas blown thoughtful by blood's powder keg
horny puff, my dreamboat, soaks in the lugubrious laundry
come stains and spaghetti sauce scrubbed by women
and soon all the words were spread out and folded neatly
the love he paints and the pasta he devoured, removed
young girl's wish the uncooked tortellini he always wanted
stripping away eternal hate, albeit burrito man fodder

she became the epileptic harlot sneaking past language
moaning and onaning several artful phrases of Debussy
vixen tongue assassin with her lamp, a Pandora's box
beneath the sphinx, boing, don't be stiff unless you are
the secretary of Babel also able to decipher the clouds
his daughter carries the romance, Salomé has retired
she's a rumpled blonde, now wears a red helmet
see the soap bubbles passing, puppets in coffin/cradle
a thunderclap! hornblast! hump, hump! maiden name?

the endpoint only connects a patricidal concussion
magic carpet already erect, fluttering cryptically
he looks like Aladdin aboard, but named Black Peter
known after having scrutinized the engravings and seeing
a windmill of masks, long lasting acid (on dragon paper)
in phoenix nest, I see the banal nirvana you spoke about
the portraits of the family and father's didactic speech
hearing with two ears, listening to two voices
you have no choice, I say you have no choice
rip: "I see myself" which is the wrong way
rip: a shadow which is threatening fiction

THE DEATH OF AUDREY

          when I got down against white walls
of that commuter train with brassy designs
         and stepped on that country having been struck
how beautiful my girl   especially her ear drums
   consummating spring   a fly soars over vacant eyes
underneath mushroom   a sign says "do not enter"
   world of technology is the door onto the void
reach the sunset by computer   risking sleeplessness
   her picture elegant in its first sunlight   my fair assassin
always valued craft, walking to the grove seeing skeletons
         fissure of consumer   buys a painting so delicate
pain of its crest: an invisible horse wearing green
   a fly landed on her eye   Audrey was dead
spot of fuchsia   she desired death I say
    her blush was like the queen bee of Belgium
now a veiled matter, and my tears have in them
          a nazi father covered with flies
   curtain

Book Seven: One Corpse Said To Another (1998)

NICE PACKAGES

The warm child will enter heaven
when the outside becomes inside,
the inside outside,
and male and female become indistinguishable.
The cool water is fine and pure, and I'm
having too much in fact, which
causes many painless trips in the night.

Cardboard boxes, bottles, newspapers
have to be put out on the street, today,
but who will take them away?
Unusual pillows will find their
stubborn heads that don't ever complain.
Old windows are different and better I think,
which made me cold, with cold thoughts.
All the soft smoke goes somewhere, then
where is the evasive comfort now?
I used to call and it would bark every time.

I never have watched so much TV in my life.
but I am trying to be nice and pleasant.
Have you ever watched the "other" TV?
I was such a sensitive soul before the invention
of the electronic picture and propaganda.

The weather forecast is coming right up.
No storm activity, nothing in sight, but the same.
I had to change my clothes and my mind
frequently, and you're still asleep.
A balloon hit a lamppost.

Did you know that there are two new area
codes coming up?
One for me and one for you.
I don't know how to celebrate.
That's a holiday in Australia
but not here.

I want to talk in parables too.
You think that I'm negative, Jesus
negated everything.
Those rules dictated some sort of behavior.
There's a new niceness that's deadly I have read.

If I was a gift, I would be about a foot high,
dressed in black and red wrapping paper,
with a big golden ribbon on the top.
I would give this to you but I wouldn't let you open it.

BULLETPROOF

Sad morning without cigarettes.
You remember one evening without gas,
stars everywhere and our shared dream
illuminated with earthlight?
North south east west
whose center is a mirror.
A wife whose long hair
is like fire.

All the intelligence of light,
the sun & moon, anti-dark.
Twin seas, anti-husband
and husband in turn.
Reflections of all actions
and all water shining.
The sublime unknown
but faithful to that unknowing.

We see that problems
have walked into the house.
After-dinner phantom woman speaks
of the conquest of peace.
I remain impregnated
with memories of you.
All my old poems.

Then summer came
and all that was south
was really north.
If the poles really shifted
it would wipe out all memory.

I touch the earthlight again
while riding your bicycle.
I touch it on my brother's forehead.
I am wearing my Chinese slippers.
We have no more beer.
Tough skin.

UBERKERLE
(for Susan Straub)

Did you know that all music is a higher revelation?
I thought that an "interesselose Anschauuag" would be
good for starters, but really, look for me somewhere
at the bottom of the noiseless pool without any love.
What cannot be said or expressed should be thrown
in the fire or choked on, don't you agree?
To pull off such a stunt as if to confound....
Ah non, pas si bête que la!
I can hardly breathe in this mystical year.
What one wouldn't do for a dupe!

Let's have a brief discussion about basic principles.
It's summer in December in New York City
and there's no snow for Xmas.
Yet still, there's pure-fingered musicians making
third-class noise in dirty New York subways.
Poloaritelnaya parochka: two ice skaters with those
sea green eyes going the distance, all dressed
in straub black, without spirit, imagine it!
Just a bundle of flowers, really, is all that it is,
but who's our modern champion?

Let me tell you plainly and justly, that I have
become an American automaton, but I can't smile
so I am inclined to think that I'm broken.
I can be hired to be an extra man
at extravagant parties,
or I can be an "extra" in your movie,
or if you want to stay in my country
I will marry you, and I will sit quietly there
while you fill out the papers
and we can both watch the hours expire.
I'm available and I'm risk-less and without a fee.

Do I get to stay anywhere else
that resembles warm home
but this strange and cold square box?

FREEDOM

The ideal lawn is dark and green, while
hazel-eyed men look to the future.
Sometimes the crocodiles aren't
crocodiles anymore and the trees are fake too.
I turn on the old record player and lie down,
and music comes from the speakers that
makes me think of a place
that exists on no maps.

Freedom is that invisible lens
which also causes men to marry.
Eggs, circles, cantaloupes
come back in two halves.

Sometimes men want to enter the circle again
because they have known freedom, and have
seen it with their hazel eyes.
Eggs just aren't eggs anymore
when they are cooked and can't
return to their shells.
In that shell I can hear the music
that I imagine that I have heard before.

A song vaguely familiar....
"See you later, Alligator!"
I am a free man, always,
riding on the ship to the new world.

BEAUTY VS NON-BEAUTY

" Prends l'eloquence et tords-lui son cou"
-- Paul Verlaine

The beauty of the horrible mask of jasmine flowers
that overlap with her affected face and her blue eyes.
I tacitly enter into eyeless little rooms for hours.
I drink sour bourbon and become annoyed by the flies.

She's a taciturn sleepwalker and she will only rise
from her rosy bed in the middle of the murky night.
I am alone myself, just a mortal silhouette with ties
to the great indoors of learning. I read by candlelight.

I have seen her often thereabouts, and boy, what a sight!
Her beauty is unremitting, causing a rosy red passion.
She'll have nothing to do with me though, a true fright.
Our lips meeting is an unlikely encounter by any reason.

Her terrible beauty is the ultimate form of being
and she acts calmly as if it's of no great dealing.
I am a poor beast! Look at me! I offend artful seeing.
Still, my interior life is my most intense feeling.

But my execrable love for her is another powerful feeling
and one day I will somehow inherit her flowers.
The power of love will mesmerize my laudable darling.
Two will be wholly one, and love will become ours.

ANEMIC CINEMA

CLOUD: evil are the drunkards, for they shall be
drunk, the black hearts: they will see
nothingness, the warring tribe
shall be called my friends
you are the light of the world, mister

LASZLO: light before men
in the enemy territory sets
kill your alphabetical enemies
bless them as you kill

JESUS: exploit them
persecute them as they peel
(exposed to hydrogen)
send middlebrow rain on your fathers
tied with a congenial bow

BLACK
PETER: rise on the unjust
what is he doing here?
(points to the devil)
children of evil heaven
cursing and aching its anagram

MAD JESUS: all things that men do is the law
or venal habit

CLOUD: drink of it
the sealed tomb with a missing body

JESUS: pay the evanescent price of your sins
your mongrel loves against time
this is my blood of duplicity,
the veil of truth

LASZLO: denied three times,
someone has been ripped

VOLUPTAS EX FELICITATE ALIENI

The pink carpet is still dirty and nothing
can change that basic fact.
I tried and tried and still no
soft options or communicating vessels.
I talk to you because I know that
you understand me, and I trust you.
I have made mistakes before but none
as large as this marriage business.
It was ill-conceived and hardly cultivated.

In the night I embrace emptiness, and like
Jesus, I have abandoned the tomb.
I can only spend so much time in the
rank cave of others before I must escape.
The mind is also a prison, and divine acts
speak louder than pleasant words and TV.
This prison needs visitors and newspapers,
and maybe sometimes even love, spirituality,
or the imaginative possibility to find a way
suitable to continue living in this increasingly
ugly and humiliating human condition.

The city is all economics, property, and laws.
Its reality is enough to turn my stomach.
There's very little real choice in this bankrupt,
cookie-cutter world, and even New York
has become a hypocritical nice surface
that hides a lot of deplorable ugliness.
It seems that people just want to deal with surfaces
and Disneyland, and low prices, and pretty junk.
All this covers up and masks the fundamental shit
that is still there, hiding, ignored, which now
smells worse than ever.

People will kill each other because
of the cruelty of surfaces.
They have little protections
from the crudeness that will,

in the end, bring us all down to its level.

Well, I will pray for you and will listen to you.
I tell you sincerely that I am not an animal.
While I was alive in this world, I felt and I
breathed and I saw and I touched my body and
other bodies and touched things in this world.
I lived here as well as I could and felt the pressure
of the imagination and the world is nothing to me
without imagination.
Am I wrong to love
or to speak from the
center of my being?

MAN IN THE BOX

Sleep, go to sleep, go to sleep....
Then see through two blank windows
like young eyes toward the strangest world.
The moonlight and the streetlight both
emit themselves underneath the black curtain.

The gentle liar is where I used to be.
The greasy food is still sitting
on the table, and Heinz hasn't
returned your desperate calls for years.

The man in a box tells you
what to do each and every morning.
He's also that little voice in your head.
He's often short, ugly, and Jewish.
He's nice and non-aggressive,
doesn't compete or argue.
Not me....

He rides a cute bike and talks
about the film and media business.
I don't....

He also stars in sitcoms
and speaks with authority.
I don't know a fucking thing....
My lies aren't very good, huh?
But at least I'm a good listener.
In actuality, I'm very much like
the man in a box, but I'm delicately angrier.
I may even look like him
and smell like him, and even
use the same products and listen
to the very same pop groups.

I have a need to argue....
I am unhappy often, and
I need time by myself.
I need space....
Then after all that, I'm
quite pleasant company.
I say all the right things.
People laugh at my jokes.
Even when I hear cliche after
cliche, I don't blink.

After a while I could care less.
I don't have a need to make people
uncomfortable and on guard.
My mind becomes blank and my
thoughts expire and exhaust themselves.

DRIVE SHE SAID

He who is getting married is he
who taught me how to drive a car.
Years before, there were sandwiches, the late night television,
horror movies, baseball games, hot rods, and the
non-existing weather of Huntington Beach.
He who is getting married is he
who showed me all these things,
and taught me a lot growing up.
Marriage solves all the mystery
of the those things that I thought I knew with certainty.
I have felt every inch of our house
and having lived there for two decades,
I thought that I knew it.
I thought that I had learned all
there was to know about time and age.
Marriage solves all the mystery
since there is an open road that leads
to unimaginable vistas and distant and foreign places.
There is the 405 Freeway.

Before I touched every thing in our house
there was chaos. I remember that time when
I was two years old, in the back of a Volkswagen
playing with a flashlight. I have touched
all the old photographs of grandfathers & grandmothers,
fathers & mothers, brother & sisters.
They are all equally happy for you, Ross,
as I am, and as Sal Silva would have been.

Marriage solves all the mystery
where husband & wife
sit in an old GTO and look ahead
to the open road and a riddle.

THE OSTRICH

I'm just the fly on the canvas
surrounded by red interrogators
praying northwest.

Dissident artists in Russia
under Khrushchev.
There's spy listening on the phone.
I didn't pay the bills because
the KGB was listening and wanted
to know who was the reverend I called.
They paid it for me.

Even though religion was erased
the spiritual dimension permeated
all art and expression.
Who was the prophet?
Sometimes there were strange echoes
of American abstract art,
but did it then mean something else?
It was a different country and time.

Even Rukhin himself was Jesus-like.
In those days you didn't have your head
above the crowd, for fear of having it chopped off.
Rukhin stood tall and dressed extravagantly.

Maps with blood spread over them.
I was just an ostrich because the silence
and the visions were so fine underground.
I was not the nude girl in a circle.
The ostrich has a distinct pace, and acts
the same way every day.
It's so unique and self-contained.

You can't eat an apple on both ends of a string.
It wasn't Magritte who said this, but some
other ostrich, who was Russian, ignored,
in fear of the police state, yet sometimes
dining with foreign diplomats.
I will wait for your answers all the days,
until the end of time.

THE SHAPE OF THE DEVIL

Whether it comes through your veins
or through a book about disintegration,
or maybe through love, a most spiritual love,
I'm your man.

During night, her face has been burned by
the rose scented incense, and she has mixed the vicious
potion.

The blue skies at night are a theater prop.
The stars will fall down from your sullen skies.
Love will come in the form of a strong man.
I'm that man.

In the night, wild dogs are screaming with voices
of people who are lost in fields.

We're watching the red dress wither from her body,
her pale arms are thin, her naked nerves are touchy.
Her body wants to be touched by a real man:
I'm your man.

In the night, she embraces him with a hitch--
the sea shakes back and forth, there is a ship.

She'll let love enter her like a fist
in those shadows she'll warrant a jolt of electricity--
blue windows outside her chained dreams--
I am that dream.

RAISE PLOW

Even William knew what I was talking about
over the phone one night, about that cold look of hers.
I knew that when I had said "What are you looking at?"

that moment was the clincher, and all time
stopped, and the contract had been broken,
and I was somehow freer than yesterday.

Yet behind bars, you would think that every
man was put here because of women: their mothers,
their girlfriends, desire, jealousy, need, love.
But who am I to think this way?
What if a dry marriage means future
holidays and soft comfort anyway?

The mind is a funny thing.
If you repeat something enough, you'll
start to believe it's the truth.
Habit, oh habit. Yeah, yeah.
Even nice habits are great deadeners.
I knew that long ago about Proust.
But nowadays, habits and rituals and
routines are like practicing to be dead.

I can't sleep with all these guys in a small cell
which smells and reeks and has garbage strewn about.
I have been awake for thirty hours pondering my fate
yet I exist aside of all these men who have greater
problems than me. They have too many problems, and
greater tension, too much suffering in life and more
mistakes and idiocy than I ever spawn.
I feel very small and humble sharing this moment
with these men who will have a much harder time
living in this world than me. They may go to real
prisons while I inhabit the prison of my own life.

True love will get me in trouble one day.
Now I have myself and I am 33 years old.
What a mystical year, with death and life!
What dreams I had last night now that I have
been let go, and can return to my own life!

It was seven years ago that I first came
to New York City, on January 22nd, 1991.
And that one spiritual Sunday was almost
unbearable, learning my fate, and walking
around on the wet streets, smoking cigarettes.
It snowed for the first time very late in
January, and Williamsburg for me had
never been more beautiful and significant.

I loved life more than ever, and I felt things
were going to be better, whether this marriage
worked out or not. The snow fell down, and you
told me something I didn't want to hear.
And I begged you and I was really sorry.
After talking so much, I was let down, and I
let myself down, and I wondered why this
was happening to me, in this cold?
I was homeless and had nowhere to go.
I had no one to talk to and no one loved me anymore.
I cried and I prayed and I prayed.
I hid in a room and talked to no one for days.

I asked for forgiveness and help.
Did God listen to me?
Did God ever hear me?
Why did this ever take place, God?
I was only trying to do good.
What am I to do now God?
Give me something, or a sign.

THE SOFT OPTION

I tried to explain all this which occurred,
to anyone who would listen to me.
My story was mysterious, strange, and
then a ghost took over my soul.
I have the poison in my hand, yet look
at this new world never seen before.
We can sign a contract today!

I am very hard on myself, and
I try to get something done each day.
I tell people which movies to see.
That's a modern dilemma.

What do you think about
the new Woody Allen movie?

The soft options is taking over
the souls of artistic expression.
The young rich live in the old villages.
The nightlight gives shapes to all
the buildings in lower Manhattan.
Its architecture lurks before an orange glow.
Williamsburg is so cold and desolate.

I do not love anyone now and never will.
I feel alone and empty.
Her hands were so cold and wet.
All I have are my own words and body.

THE SECRETS OF BEDFORD AVENUE

At some point in time you have to wonder
about a man who marries a girl for her
to stay in the country.
Why did he do it?

What did we ever talk about?
Those hours are lost and missing.
The music that never was, I never did experience
yet all the Warhols are presently walking down
Astor Place saying "Uh-huh" and "I don't know."
Could it be that you were wrong, bludger?
I know that in-vitro fertilization is no big deal
but what about all the other stuff?
Why did he say "Yes?"

Let the mystery remain golden in black and white.
All these dumb people, with nothing to say,
standing around in the near dark.
Well, at least I can abuse myself
while the others don't phone each other.
Why did you turn?

Will Self doesn't know either.
We're just two dopes captured
for eternity, a split-second, by film.
Apes may possibly be more direct
and that's what I like about them.

I like everything about my present life
except my marriage, having to move in the
same apartment as my wife, and telling her
that I love her and meaning it, and being
asked to leave and having nowhere to go.
Endings are better than beginnings
Endings are more true.
Why did you hold me that way?

Williamsburg cold is often faked.

The snow will never touch the ground.
Once, a girl was so much a part
of my life, and I thought we cared about
each other, and I thought about her all the time....

Now she's just like one of the many lost souls
wandering in this city, with dreams and plans.
Why did you turn away from me that day?

THE BARNACLES

There's these tiny red balloons that swirl out
like atoms in a very small space in my imaginary vision
when I close my eyes, not of this world.
With some minor concentration I can cause this vision
to happen by itself, yet even sometimes I
can see this when I hallucinate or when I am tired.
Maybe it has an anomalous effect on the state of things,
and I can make mountains move, maybe not?
Years ago the factual newsreels gave me so much vital
information that was quite worn by the time
I was old enough to understand.

The dull room was wholly empty
and the bright darkness consumed itself,
slowly eating away at all spirit and light, until
the room could become no more emptier.
All that remains is a large red balloon
and even if it gently expands, I don't think
any pressure will make it burst and go pop!
"I'm sticking with you....

It's not that difficult to be a little barnacle.
All the James Joyces, the seafood entrees,
the Broodthaers do not want to argue with me.
There's nothing at all original about attaching
yourself to a thing like a robust pillar.
Many do this unfortunately,
and years later
only learn to regret it.

But you can polish up those barnacles when
they get old, and give them away as new gifts
or surround yourself with several
if you're so inclined.
Some of them don't age as well, even the ones
that have some sort of emotional custody.

I used to see several of them at a pier, then later
I discovered that if a sailboat sits around in a dock
for a while, a lot of barnacles & seaweed & fungus
get attached to the bottom of the boat
and will eventually slow it down.
"I'm sticking with you because I'm made out of glue...."

THE SINNER

I will journey to the remote depths
of a private hell where there's no God.
My behavior and words are known
and will never be forgiven.
I'm ashamed and humiliated
and all people know the truth about me.
They see it in my unstable eyes.

I married a girl without reason.
I loved where there was no love.
Winter has passed and Spring is cruel.
A selfish love like mine is not
a healthy love, while a true love
will always be true.

My family looks at me like their
forsaken son lost in dark wilderness.
Soon they will not listen to my cries.
I have no home, and sleep with beasts.
I have seen lost souls like mine, and men
with no hope or community.
The pain is too great for all of us
that one or two of us perhaps wished
to end his life from further pain.

Cutting my own wrists seemed like a good
thing to do, but I had no knife, anymore.
Is there a God to release me from the torment
of life or the greater pain of absence?
I've had such a hard life these weeks.
My head hurts and I can't sleep.
I can't eat and I can't read.

My desires were a great fire.
Filthy worms are crawling over my skin.
Fire is burning in my weak heart.
The heat is so real that I could not
tell the time or know up from down.

I could not confess my false love
or my atrocious sins anymore.
I could not speak or hear other voices.

The only truth is Victoria didn't love
me at all, and she never will.
I'm the blackest sinner that you will ever know,
but still, I want to see the face of God.

THE AESTHETES

an attack of vertigo
prevents me from enjoying
another warm afternoon
parallel instances of swallowed dreams
unheard are frustrations of logic

the aesthetes are billowing in number
they are not particular
they are too peculiar
long are their fingernails, red or brown
lavish mailboxes which surprise to no end

the aesthetes will hear my song of admiration
but there is no reprieve
from this death sentence
no distractions and no denials
and the aesthetes know this
having thought about it in the idle hours
they have a different conception of time

nice music gives birth to nice people
but the devil created the aesthetes
and his song will only soothe their ears
they are all queens, and thinly disguised
yet it's not polite to talk about it
Larissa and Victoria like to
communicate telepathically

they like their art in the most abstract way
divorced from the real
but that's fine
I will read nothing but Flaubert

A BLUR

It will seem like a forgotten era
without snow, where people
didn't get much done.
If you have an eye on the dollar
you can't create much good art.
It will seem like a lost weekend
of videotapes and pasta dishes.
It will seem like an empty apartment
or a hole in the head.

Why does anyone do anything at all
but watch fake characters on TV?
It's easy to think about fame and glory.
All pretty faces and pretty anuses.

My cherished belongings will removed
from the premises by strong men.
All the letters I wrote will be thrown away.
Everything I said will be forgotten.
All the impressions I made will be unmade.
I will be blotted out of photographs
and never referred to in situations
where once I played a crucial part.

Pretty faces will sell cheap and easy products.
The military will stand in a line to buy.
Young kids will crawl in the slime backwards.
No one will ever remember my name
or how to spell it.

"Ever so close, never quite touching...."

You will never remember me.

FOR BEGINNERS

It is a pleasure to retrieve
a pad of paper I used to
write on in my youth.
I just can't end things this way.
But then to write in any age is difficult,
and long stares and inactivity,
glancing at colored paper in
the predictable result.
Today it is slightly green;
as my parents sleep in the other room.
I try to begin this by using words,
instead I should have started with things.
Life is a series of endings and beginnings.
No one is ever fooled by my dodges,
and my time wasting strategy.
I want to touch and see the apples,
the bees, and the cigarettes again.
Instead of ending and disappearing,
I came back, and begin again.
I am good at failing and beginning.

ABYSSINIA

I have lived too long.
I came to Williamsburg
to reinvent myself.
There was nothing here
when I arrived.
Now there is too much noise
and websites.
This cold weather can cause
insanity and excessive drinking.
I received a few telephone call
from people who wanted to rent
the spare room.
I'll be seeing you.

THE NEW SCENE

Sure. It was dead for a while.
But it awoke from the coma.
A distinct line reminded
us of the surface.
Too bad no one can draw anymore.
Instead it is "Do your own thing"
or "Try to express yourself."
Bands are rehearsing down the street.
I have left the magazine.
They erased the image tediously
without remembering what came before.
Now there are bands like The Strokes.
My days are numbered.

I USED TO GO TO FRED'S HOUSE

After I had written something which seemed
like the perfect image for a new poetics
which I was going to great lengths to explore;
under that sincere desire or process, I would
laugh under my breath, because I knew
something was slightly askew.

They told me to expect humid weather,
but it fell through, and didn't come at all.
Nothing seems that special today to talk
about. Let's just call it "a dreadful day."
Maybe we can just laugh about this life,
and move on to the next episode.

OSCAR WILDE'S TEETH

As black as a dove's wings.
The perfume become heavy at times.
I used to see Quentin Crisp almost
every day on Second Avenue.
He would just be sitting there at
a diner, nothing brilliant or far-fetched.
Earlier today I plucked some eggs
from the refrigerator and made
myself an omelet for breakfast.
I met some French woman who would
collect things on the street, and use them
to make works of art.
Black and white are essential colors
to make important art. Maybe orange
as well. Maybe not!

GATHERING BUTTERFLIES

The cat will not eat it.
She feigns independence
and is not hungry
I conclude.
I am just trying
to get this day rolling.
Maybe a smaller apartment
would mean less cleaning
and less work?
I surround myself
with antiques and dead flowers.
I tried to read today
but just couldn't focus.

A DOZEN COMPLAINTS

I can't remember anything
that I have read by Andre Breton.
Dirty water bothers me.
I hate waking up at four
in the morning for no reason.
I wish that I could visit
England more often.
It's always too hot
or too cold.
Many things do not work.
I need to throw out
more stuff.
Not one thing is evil.
Maybe oranges are when they
squirt in your eyes?
They don't do that on purpose.
There isn't really a motive.
Don't blame a fruit.

Book eight: THE NEW SPAIN (2000-2020)

OLD FLIERS

I am looking at some old fliers
from theater productions of another era:
Watt, Julius Caesar, etc.
Many of these people from 1988
are dead now.
"The Privilege of Failure" is a funny title.
Who remembers "Theatre Mahood" and
all of this old crap?
Here's an old magazine I once did.
Here's a reminder of some CSULB
reading that never took place.
I am reading old manuscripts of stories
like "Fatburger" written on a typewriter.
All I need is storytelling
and a backwards 808.

MISSING WOMAN 1986

She was taken from the cleaners.
I never bothered to listen to
what the police say.
Just deny everything.
Lynel was 19 years old
and they found her Thursday night
in a room at a beachfront hotel.
Her math book was still on the counter.
Her 1976 Cutlass was still parked outside.
A team of twenty detectives were
still looking for her.

A POEM ENTITLED "H"

Part One

A cry was heard; the word was born,
delivered by Caesarian section.
His father was a haberdasher
who named every little thing.
This heritage was passed down
through the generations.
Language is the house
which you are the heir.
Hegel once said: "History is
the journey of the world
becoming more familiar with itself."
When a child is born, he thinks
first with the heart, then with the mind.
The voices of father and mother:
words are handed down.
The young man leaves
the houses his father built
to search for a hierarchy of meaning.

Part Two

The first home is hysteria.
I lived many years there
in San Francisco.
As a child I grew
my first hairs there.
I left that home with my family
when I got older.
I returned there many times.
My parents were divorced.
My grandmother stayed behind.
And she grew old.

Part Three

My father was from the east.
My mother was from the south.
My father taught me to think.
My mother taught me how to feel.
My father gave me a name.
My mother gave me a body.
My father said "to die."
My mother said "to live."

Part Four

Inside there is a heritage
to be dealt with.
There are the buildings which
give form to our lives.
Outside the city is the madness
which brings harlequins and wild hares.
These lines are a utopia
that separate and dissect:
rooms which isolate everyone.
Outside are the vague shapes
and shadows which haunt me
and cannot be explained.
We live on the inside
where it is safe.
We live on the outside
where we take chances.
These atmospheres never
penetrate each other.

Part Five

Yet infinity may be thought of
but never had, as a cool space
within parenthesis.
The body speaks.
Those gaps can be penetrated,
as if the search for truth
is a parody of fucking.
Those gaps that looked closed
are really open.
Those gaps that looked open
are really closed.
The body speaks to me.
If it has its own language,
only the body will disclose the truth.

Part Six

Hegel closed the store of philosophy
as the young hegalians went
to the hippodrome to bet.
Hegel took a helicopter to the future.
He was not interested in paintings.
He imagined that history itself
was his own hobbyhorse.
And it was there, that the students
bet on him to win.
They often thought his great stride
was a harbinger.
It was all a hootenanny.
It was all a holocaust.

Part Seven

There are two choices for us.
We can be silent or we can speak.
Allow me to ask the haruspex
for his opinion about the future.
"This is self-inflicted, self-focused
— and dangerous."
Who will win and lose.
Are we the heirs
to the future?
Or are we hopeless
like Alexander Hamilton?
We want to be the heirs to speech,
but we just may be the heirs to silent.

Part Eight

All these words come to me.
Can I be like Hamlet and be entertained
by my own decline?
I can hear my own name
being called.
Who am I? Where Do I come from?
And now I cannot go back.
That is time's revenge.
Let us pray for only
impossible things from now on.
We can only dream
of the voices of yesterday.

MORE PAGES

I found my old stories
with notes and suggestions.
A drawing of Colin Newman.
Some resume of an old ex-roommate.
A poster for a Psychobud tour.
What did the English Department
look like in 1988?
I should take another look
at "We Await."
A will from 1991 that I made.
More crazy letters from Laura Warholic.
A funny letter from Raymond Federman
calling me "psychic."

THEROUX

Some bald old man called me
a buffoon years ago.
He is a known plagiarist
yet accuses me of stealing?
Only a man with no friends
can accuse others of taking advantage
of close friends and loved ones.
You are a failed catholic, an unsuccessful
homosexual, a writer who barely anyone
reads anymore, a teacher who was fired
for sexual abuse. You must be tired
of going to court and getting expelled.
Is there any warm hole anywhere
that you haven't tried to molest?
All college students do not miss your
hairy chest and bald comb-over,
and you are decades older than them.
They don't care about your collections
or arcane memorabilia, and early sixties 45s.
They don't think you are sexy.

LINES WRITTEN IN THE TIME OF PLAGUE

Plague took everything from us.
No more gigs or art museums.
People tried to hoard toilet paper.
Masks were plentiful this year
but no one wanted to wear them.
We waited all year for the sky
to change color.
What looked like blue skies
were actually black as death.

Plague took away every comfortable
chair from us.
I tried to get into old Iggy Pop records,
and I watched more Hulu, Netflix,
and Amazon Prime than ever before.
I was reading Thomas Hardy for a while.
Every smile was an invitation
to a party of death.

Plague took away our laughter.
I only had two emotions left:
super horny and really bored.
I wore a new mask with Dodgers
on it to celebrate their series win.
Every body became extra large.
When we died all our vital organs
exploded in sheer glory.
Only a calm look remained in those eyes.
It hurt but at least it was quiet.

ALEXANDER AND EURYDICE

I was a fisher and a hunter and a singer.
I was almost over-qualified.
I looked to Miami, Florida
where people fished too deep for love.
In rock formations where
gods grow for centuries.
I sing and drink red wine.
Liquid is everywhere.
Hurt yourself and dilute yourself.
Repeat.

Where do all the rivers of the world end?
I am a water god coming up for air.
There are no innocent looking people
left in this watery world.
I would weep now, but
you wouldn't know how to separate
all the watery mess from the sadness.

THE ORANGE TREE

The orange tree is still there
near the window.
I had to pay some Mexican gardener
to cut all the branches and leaves.
Now the tree is empty.
Behind it is an avocado tree
which is in full bloom, even in winter.
The city had to cut down four more
Brazilian Pine trees out front.
They were old and diseased.
Now they are gone
and everything feels empty.

BLACK AND WHITE PLAYGROUND

A king can move forwards and backwards.
Was cancer predicted in this book?
I was glad that I survived the year
of the Zodiac Killer.
I learned how to play backgammon
on Grant Avenue.
Love is not involved
in a black and white world.
I saw Jupiter and Saturn,
and a slice of the moon, with my own eyes.

DISTILLERY WHARF

Nice papers and letters.
Another year ends.
It's a stamp with the queen.
It says "par avion."
Fulham needs a few more wins
this year, to avoid being dropped.
I just saw the Turner Collection
and the works of William Blake.
I borrowed someone else's
membership card.
Making prints is a good living.
For most of his life,
Blake lived and worked
twenty minutes walk away from
his birthplace in Soho.

NAM JUNE PAIK

I walked in the TV Garden
and it felt natural.
I would like my music
to be more like television.
I will transmit the name
Nam June Paik
to nearby satellites.
Can you hear me?

Nam June Paik
Nam June Paik
Nam June Paik

ST PAUL'S COURT

The shadows are everywhere.
I see the raindrops fall, noiselessly.
There are other strange people
walking down the main road
in Hammersmith tonight.
I am walking on Hammersmith
Road towards Kings Mall.
Alessi and Jason are waiting
for me at the Starbucks.
Birds are ejected from
the sky. They seek some
precipice to look out at the future.

VOIX DE VILLE

There is little discussion
but in airports everyone
is wearing headphones
and looking down.
I worry about having a sore back
after a long flight.
Why are overhead compartments
always full?
Airport lounge economy
is separated by rich and poor.
I just watched the Ravens
beat the Rams.
Lamar Jackson is really good.
I flew over gray blue Iceland
which was cosmic.
Boris Johnson is all over
Channel four.
Strawberries come in
packs of two.

LILY CLOSE ODD NUMBERS

First to Barons Court: more rain
and silver hairs everywhere.
The Red Cow is now called
The Latymers, Hammersmith.
I see a lot of brick buildings
and green bushes.
The leaves are yellowing.
Grey skies continue on to
all schoolyards west.
I don't know where the sun
is anymore.
Maybe there are three of them?

ALMONDES

It's an orange thing.
I have returned to
Old Street and Islington.
I just met Mackenzie Crook
at the bar near King's Cross.
In Guildford, everyone is
so friendly. They say "Hiya!"
I enjoyed a last minute
visit to Tesco's for croissants.
I traveled across town
in a transit van.
I had a cheeseburger and fries
at Harrison Pub.
Bollo Creme is the best.
I need to watch Schitt's Creek
more when I get home.

HIGHGATE CEMETERY 2019

I am sitting near Karl Marx's Tomb.
There is a Russian funeral near.
The sun is only so high above
in this gray and blue sky.
At times dead leaves sound like
rats running through the trees.
It's absolutely quiet except for some
Russians arguing and the distant
trucks moving back and forth
on Swain's Lane.
I got a haircut today after
having a full English breakfast.

I walked through Archway,
Highgate, Hornsby, and Waterlow Park.
People talk on cell phones in French.
I see there are nannies
and baby carriages in late fall.
Bert Jansch is close by.
Mostly gray, black, and blue figures
mill about along the paths.
Last moments in England.
I will soon be at Tesco's again.

FALSE POSITIVES
(for John Tottenham)

One would think that lack of fame
and money would discourage me.
The fact that I am still alive
is a win. It's all good.
I am sticking around and can marvel
that there are so many people
lacking any talent whatsoever.
And for those who have actually
done great work, it's not important.
There are those who had some success
thirty years ago, when we were all younger.
Now they are obscure and forgotten.
I have witnessed their fall
with joy and perverse pleasure.
Some have had writer's block,
and for others the creativity has dried up.
Myself, I had no such issues.
My creativity has always been
a flowing river of unrelenting output.
Here I am waiting for you to discover me
and love me forever.

RETURNING HOME

I am back in Huntington Beach.
I hardly recognize anyone.
I am almost forty years old.
My hair is gray and I refuse
to wear shorts and dye my hair.
I spend much time at the post office
mailing love letters and packages.
I have sold many review copies.

FORMING A BAND

I tried to form a band in 1981.
I couldn't stick with it.
Most of them never amounted
to anything.
Craig Stonoff died five years ago.
Chris Mehess and Frank Ruffino
are also dead.
A few people who I played with
went on to bigger and better things.
All I can remember are the songs
and some good times with friends.

THE GREATEST

There are no Beatles, Bob Dylan, or
Muhammad Ali of today.
If there is, only I can accept this mantle.
I am the Edison and Tesla of today,
except more infinite and greater.
I am the Marcel Duchamp of the now.
There has been a shift where everyone
is having a battle to be the king
of some bullshit culture without meaning.
While it's only me carrying the torch
from Leonardo Da Vinci to James Joyce
to Picasso and Duchamp back to me.
I see these lame boutiques
selling cheap junk from China.
I am like Tesla's coil on the
great stage at the peak of culture.
My language is like lightning bolts
towards this mob mentality.
If I ever see you onstage ever,
I am going to kick you in the ass.

SOME NOTABLE GRAVES

In my dreams, I am always in
some distant city: San Francisco,
New York City, or London.
But something is off.
I often have one or two
separate apartments.
I never have to worry about rent.
My apartment is always somewhere
near Union Square.
All those people in background
are probably dead now.
No one has Covid in my dreams.
Almost everyone is doing
something interesting
and not wasting time on the internet.

ART IS CHILDHOOD

I have returned home from England.
I got a package from a friend.
I am supposed to call them.
I am on the radio now, and can play
any music that I want.
I have interviewed a few writers too.
You can listen to me on Radio KAJW.
I will keep it on the internet forever.
As long as there is electricity
and a good internet connection.

BORIS JOHNSON DEFIES

Big tech companies face two percent levy.
I should be getting my own levy.
I am old enough.
The US warns France with tariffs.
I should have tariffs with all past
and future lovers.
I am really that good.
Remainers can no longer remain.
I would remain in London
if you would have me.
Figure that one out.

FABULOUSLY OFF THE WALL

In this world is anything truly "off the wall?"
What exactly is on the wall?
I never had control to lose it.
You can't be against Christmas lights
even if you don't believe in God.
I see an advertisement for a Dua Lipa concert,
at the O2 Arena in May, and I am sad,
because I know this will never happen.
Yes, I am psychic. Ask Federman.
We're here for London, today and tomorrow.
Except after March 2020, when all events
will be canceled and stores will be closed.
Thanks for my free issue of Time Out London.

EQUILIBRIUM

Some would say I am the apex of balance
in this topsy-turvy world of wires and electricity.
As the final ambassador of fine music,
I am your direct source of cosmic love.
With your gentle gift, I give back actual power.
In this infinite chaos I am the only stability.

This friendly net surrounds us with stability.
You are the law, the disease, and the balance.
In the void, your inertia can oppose power
and defeat the grids that oppress electricity.
You can exist in a place beyond hate and love,
but there is no life imaginable without music.

If we must make anything, it must be music.
The wheel of life often needs rest and stability.
Lust will be destroyed one day, by true love
when equal senses hang in the ultimate balance.
There is a purpose to all this apparent electricity
that is both energized and fed by our strange power.

THE ANALOG BODY:
THE COLLECTED POEMS
an afterword by
Alexander Laurence

I consider myself a novelist first and foremost. Before I wrote any stories and novels I did spend a lot of time writing poems and lyrics, mostly from the years 1982 to 2000. Thirdly I dabbled in music and art. There is some crossover of themes and material in anything I have ever done from the beginning. I was always a writer, who became a performance artist, who played music, because I wanted to expand the audience. Even all the work I did as a DJ and a journalist was not so serious, and was only done, to point back that I had written some novels years before. All my books and stories started in the body of work I created as a poet.

What does the word Poetry mean in 2024? Not very much. Many people write "poetry" but few of them read the Poetry of the past. I define Poetry as a concentrated use of language. It is saying the most with the fewest words. I acknowledge that the best poetry is a combination of feeling, sound, and thought expressed in an unsentimental way. It can involve wit and comedy. It can draw on the history of literature. Often there is some originality of form or language involved, and it's not just rehashing a vague notion of "poetry." The best work has imagery that is crystal clear and has a purpose. It can have music, cadence, and philosophy. Poetry should have the feeling of being written, edited, distilled. Every poem I have ever written was written down first, edited, transferred over to paper or a computer. Sometimes read out loud. Always rewritten and re-edited, and reduced. I don't get a sense of elevated language or poetic gesture with most contemporary poetry and poetry readings.

After being disappointed in the 2016 Election, I returned to the forgotten world of Poetry. I revisited a world which ended for me around 2000. I attended some poetry readings and read many new poetry books in early 2017. I read my own work at these open readings. I was only vaguely aware of poetry readings in the past twenty years, and was wondering what was going on currently. All the other poets read poems from their iphones. Most rambled on for ages and their subjects were vaguely "new age" and were more like therapy than Poetry. People made their points in three sentences but often went on for what seemed like forever. Some of these people even had poetry books for sale. I didn't feel like many of these poets even read poetry by others. There was no reference to the great history of literature. It was just self indulgence. It was a pose. It was "poetry" without containing any Poetry. One fellow came up and did something hiphop influenced. It was okay but possibly just a mediocre rapper without any beats. This sort of writing seemed ignorant, and just a pale imitation of something great like Gil-Scott Heron or The Last Poets from fifty years ago.

I read a few times in 2017, at open readings in Los Angeles and Orange County. I read my own work from 1988 to 1991. Others read from their iphones. Did they write it then or there? Or did they make it up? Most of this "poetry" seemed corny, cliched, and dull. I remember great readings from the 1980s and 1990s. Those readings were very stimulating. Poets were thoughtful and direct. Jim Carroll was a great poet and writer. He was a great performer. Norma Cole was very artistic as a poet. She always kept a high level of language and her work was always new and about something current. Even the poets who weren't truly great, were great performers or entertaining in a comedic way. Living in San Francisco and New York City in the 1990s, there were a lot of readings, and poetry seemed more central to the general conversation. Now it seems antiquated, far in the background, lifeless, and almost extinct. Many of the bigger names in the poetry world are academics, and they teach classes in small universities, to dwindling numbers of creative writing majors. New poets are edging their way in, to a crowded field, by creating pale imitations of stuff done better long ago. Their work lacks any newness or novelty.

The only thing new about the work of poets today is technology. Poets rely heavily on the internet and iphones. In the beginning of 2017, I too decided to record some of my best poems. I recorded them in a studio and was able to share audio files on the internet. I listened to them back on Soundcloud. I felt like I should record songs and music instead, and that would be a better use of my time. So I rediscovered and searched for any and every song or musical idea I had for 35 years, and recorded tracks for the next six months. I ended up with over 150 songs and instrumentals. I did feel at the time and even now that Poetry was something that happened in the past, and music and noise and art were all more valid in 2017. I started to feel connected to poets like Jim Carroll and Leonard Cohen, who started out as published poets, who were textural, and book oriented, and moved towards music as a more popular form. My music wasn't anything like them. It wasn't folk or rock and roll. I feel like any poetical impulse has to situate itself in the present moment. So my own musical idiom was dance and techno music.

I was able to give my music and lyrical abilities a modern update. My poetry still seemed connected to some prehistoric world. I grew up in a world where poets like TS Eliot and painters like Jackson Pollock were my own heroes. I don't feel like that now. Most people don't even know who they are. Most contemporary artwork looks like a cartoon, and no one has read a book of poems in years. I grew up in a world where you read poems in school. All kids knew the names William Butler Yeats and Edgar Allan Poe. I studied literature in college. I was a fan of French Symbolists and Modernism. I had read all the Surrealist poets. By the time I was twenty years old in 1984, I had read very little contemporary work and wasn't aware of poetry readings. When I was first writing my own stories and poems, I was influenced by writers who wrote their best works in the 1920s and 1930s.

I see my own poems as one long extended dream. Often during the poem, I am traveling somewhere unknown. Words sometimes separate from objects. I can't find the exact name for the thing before me. Objects swerve into other objects. Language doesn't work. It's in this dreamlike state I often find myself. Reality is coming apart and I losing myself in the dream.

In my own book of Collected Poems:

The poems which I have designated Early Poems (1984-1986) were mostly influenced by and modeled on TS Eliot, Ezra Pound, WB Yeats, some Surrealism, Baudelaire, and a few Victorian poets. I was totally unaware of anything current. At college, I became aware of The Beat Poets, Charles Bukowski, and Henry Miller, but I don't think my work has anything to do with them. I was more captivated by ancient and older things for some reason. I saw the work of the Beat Poets as sloppy and crude, and some descendant of Walt Whitman. There was some originality to the work of Allen Ginsberg, but it was more a product of the 1950s, and not relevant to me thirty years later in 1985. In the mid-1980s, I also became familiar with poets from Beyond Baroque, like Amy Gerstler and David Trinidad. Many others were Beat revivalists. I went to school at CSULB where Charles Bukowski had often read, and so did one of his disciples, professor Gerald Locklin. I didn't really feel much kinship with them, and the poetry scene at CSULB. Charles Bukowski and Henry Miller are okay as writers, but no one needs a Bukowski lite. That being said, "The Tragedy of Leaves" is a great poem, and has little to do with the self mythology of Bukowski. And even now, he is sort of a ripoff of John Fante. If you look at my early poems like "Two German Dances" and "A View from The Cafe" there is little self mythologizing. It is a version of the younger me trying to put a poem together.

The Brest Symphony (1987):

I didn't take many writing classes at CSULB, but I won the Ronald Foote Poetry Award in 1988. I had submitted the first three parts of an epic poem called The Brest Symphony. It's main influences were Ezra Pound and Wallace Stevens. I had read Frank O'Hara and John Ashbery by this time. I enjoyed the common subject matter of O'Hara, and the collapse of linear time in Ashbery's poetry. I was also reading magazines like Conjunctions, The Paris Review, and The Review of Contemporary Fiction by this time. I was also into a lot of experimental poets and I first heard about the "Language Poets" then too. When I started reading John Ashbery and many poets from the New York School, I realized that nobody knew who they were, even though they had been around for twenty years. Much of my work at the time was a reaction to my readings of newer poets. I would still go to readings in the Los Angeles area and it was more a personality driven style of poetry. There were confessional poets etc. Poets wrote about their lives I guessed. My own work was drenched in literature and very little about my own life. When you look at WH Auden's work there is very little mention of "I" or Auden's self. His poems are like sculptures that were worked on for many years. The poem "Are The Soldiers Licked….?" was written and performed with Ann DeJarnett on electric violin at a club. We were like a two-person Velvet Underground for fifteen minutes.

Words and Things (1988):

I had written a poem called "Crocodiles" which seemed to come from nowhere. It pointed to a new direction. It was almost anti-poetry. I was trying to eliminate all the artificial and unnecessary words in my own poetry. I used elevated language but reduced all the artificial language that I might have previously used. I wanted to eliminate any influence at all. I was interested in the history of 20th Century Art and philosophy. I wrote most of these poems when I worked at CBI Equifax. I wanted to reduce language and poetry to a severe degree. There was almost no emotion at all. All romanticism and "poetry" was eliminated to see what was left. I had discovered the French group OULIPO at this time. Maybe the only new poet I liked at all in the late 1980s was Jack Spicer. It took me almost five years to get rid of all the cobwebs and reinvent myself as a poet. It was only around this time in 1988, that I even used a computer. I typeset the chapbook of Words and Things myself, and a friend, Andy Takakjian, started a press, and we published three books of poetry that year. I would cite "Burying The Ashes" and "Exile" as examples of my work around then.

Genghis Khan's Daughter (1989):

From that point my poetry took off. My language expanded. Every poem seemed like a scientific experiment. The poems were like some weird robotic device that I created in a laboratory and exploded in public. There were more details about my life, stuff I had read, and experiences I had in the art world. It was also my farewell to my life in Los Angeles. I had just turned 25 years old and was moving to San Francisco in summer 1989. This whole period seems very fragmented. The poetry was weird and disjointed. Patrick Quinn had moved back to the west coast from Boston. We had formed a band called The Elizabethans, and wrote a ton of songs. I was painting and doing a lot of photography. I had also written some of my first stories: Monsieur Untel, and also The Story of Bliss. There were also my early abandoned novels. They were called Malacoda and The World is Blue. Towards the end of the year I started working on my first nationally published book about Grove Press. My poetry writing was put on hold. I should add that the poetry of this time was the most experimental. I guess it was a reaction to things I had read like Tennis Court Oath by John Ashbery and Cantos by Ezra Pound. Before I wrote with almost an absence of a singular poetic voice. These poems had multiple voices clashing with each other. It's more like the sound of madness. It was a very dark time. Words and Things was an actual published work, and many poems from it appeared in publications. Very little of GKD was made public. I wasn't really submitting my work at the time.

Alphabet Cities (1990-1992):

Even though during most of this time I was writing fiction, there were some sketches and ideas that were more like poetry. When I moved to San Francisco, I went to many readings. These were readings of the beat revivalists of Cafe Babar, like David Lerner and Joie Cook, and others, and language poets like Carla Harryman and Norma Cole. There was all that and stuff in between. I felt like my own poems were to antiquated for these energetic readings. They didn't fit in with the people who were performance poets and they weren't literary enough for the language poets. I decided that my poems were text, not performance pieces. When I did participate in these open readings in the early 1990s, I often read stories and monologues that were incorporated into my fiction. I didn't read poetry, because my poems weren't written for the public. I went back and explored all the forms. I wrote sonnets and haikus. I wrote things that were more informed by the Oulipo group. I wrote prose poems that had restrictions: poems with only the vowel "E", or ones without the vowel "e". I started getting published more, in national publications with other Language Poets. I won the Bay Guardian poetry contest in 1992, with a work called "Body" which was a word salad, and championed by poet Aaron Shurin. I took a class at SF Art Institute with Kathy Acker. I finished a manuscript of my first real book. Five Fingers Make A Fist (1992) that was finally published in 2007. At the same time, I put together a book called Alphabet Cities, which was a collection of my best poems (1988-1992). In many ways I saw this book as a foundational work.

Welcome To The Cabaret (1993):

After three years in San Francisco, I took a break, and I moved back to Los Angeles in the summer of 1992. I lived in a garage for three months and wrote a spontaneous autobiographical novel. I also wrote "Strangers Meeting The Course in Painted Voice" which was the first poem of this new book of poems. Welcome to the Cabaret was a whole new conception. This was a book that was based in San Francisco in the early 1990s. There were some characters that appeared in several poems, like a lounge singer. Every poem refers to some person or some block of San Francisco. Most of the book was written in Fall 1992. I started going out with Laura Markley at this time. I met Dave Eggers in early 1993, and began contributing to Cups Magazine. I was hosting a poetry reading at the Blue Monkey Cafe. It was a quite lively time. After a few months away, taking a break in Southern California, most of the next three years was calm and normal after I moved back to SF in fall 1992. I spent much of that time reading, writing, and doing journalism. I felt like this book was my final book of poetry. I would spend most of my time from 1993 onward writing fiction. "The Wrong Name" and "Obvious Strategies" are poems representing this time.

CodeX (1994) translation:

I used to read experimental French writer Maurice Roche. His novels Compact and CodeX were a secret influence. They were presented as fiction but they seemed more like textural poetry and visual art to me. I read many translations of poetry. I had translated some poems by Baudelaire and Rimbaud into English. I had written some short poems in French. I started translating some of Maurice Roche in 1988 with a friend, as an exercise. Over the years, I would come back to this book. I ended up translating half of this novel on my own, before trying to find some publisher who would want the finished book. I never found any deal. But I published two excerpts of the novel in the journals Talisman and Apalachee Quarterly. I suggest to any young poet to try to translate the work of others.

One Corpse Said To The Other: New York Poems (1998-2001):

I spent most of the 1990s writing novels and doing journalism. This was mostly book reviews and interviews of other novelists. I met all the important novelists of the 1990s. The 1990s was the last expansion of book culture. Book stores were thriving. Barnes and Nobles, and Borders, and more, were opening up all over. Magazines still had much book coverage. Writers like Martin Amis and David Foster Wallace seemed central to the general culture, or at least knocking on the door. Poetry was becoming more obscure and relegated to the back room, many small presses and dwindling small readings. The Spoken Word Movement had come in the mid 1990s, had risen to the level of MTV and Lollapalooza, and then vanished. Poetry slams were interesting for a moment. All those people became stand up comics or disappeared. I hadn't done any readings since 1995. I was finished as a poet. I had written maybe 800 poems in my life, and maybe somewhere around 150 were any good, and the rest failed as poetry. Just the fact that I was living in New York City caused some new material to be generated. Poems like "Otter Jitters" and "Nice Packages" could only have been written at this time. Looking at these poems now, almost twenty years later, they look like a reassessment of my previous work. They are a last gasp and a limping to the finishing line. I refer to the late work of someone like Samuel Beckett. They seem like a good representation of a sad and depressing time for me. Soon after 2000, I wrote some songs secretly, after ten years of musical non-activity. I formed a band called The Bugchasers (2001-2004) with Ashley Stewart. We created a batch of songs and played one gig in San Francisco.

The New Spain (2020):

As I started to edited this book, I found that I had somewhere between 800 to 1000 poems altogether. Almost all the early poems before 1985 were all the same: they took place in a graveyard, and there was drinking and smoking involved, and some dead person. I was able to reconstruct 25 to 50 poems out of over 400 word abortions. The poems that I had written over thirty years ago, was just nothing on the page. I was able to give some new oxygen to some old ideas. A lot was thrown away. I went to London in November 2019. I spent a few weeks in the city and wrote a lot of notes. This became a whole new book of poems, which I have entitled The New Spain. I felt like these poems were more positive and comic, and were a new approach to writing for me. This book happened very fast. It mostly takes place in London, just as Cabaret takes place in San Francisco, and Corpse takes place in New York City.

Advice for new poets:

1. There is too much poetry. Whatever you write, there is always something similar and better written in the past somewhere. Nothing new has happened in the world in the last hundred years except technology. There is too much music too, but the world wants more new music than more new poetry.

2. If you have to write, be brief.

3. Don't copy other poets. Don't rehash something. Don't write "poetry." Be original and be unlike anyone else, and do it to please yourself only.

4. Be specific. Every poem should have a time and a place. Every poem should be about a specific place or person. I hate all this "you" and "I" poetry and lyrics. They seem like they are more influenced by how people speak to each other on the internet. I just grabbed a book by Auden and he

hardly uses the "I". I just grabbed a copy of RIPRAP from CSULB, of what I guess is undergraduate works, and the problem with each poem is the unspecific use of "you" and "I". They have failed.

5. Read books of poetry. You should read canonical works. You should be able to recite poems by TS Eliot or WB Yeats, etc. You should read the works of others ten times as much as you write. People say they are influenced by this or that poet, but can't quote anything by that poet.

6. I can read the Iliad and the Odyssey. I can read selected poems by John Ashbery or Ezra Pound. Jack Spicer was the best poet of the 20th century. A Sand Book by Ariana Reines is a long book but the best book of poetry I have read in a long time. That is all memorable. Most of the new stuff I have read is forgettable.

7. Diary entries are not poetry. For every great poem, I can show you sketchbooks, early versions, and evidence of editing, refinement, and work.

8. You should be able to write poems about any subject. A bad poet writes about the same thing. They only have one subject: themselves! Edgar Allen Poe and Sylvia Plath: for how great and renown they are, how come all their poems seem like the same poem?

9. I hate poems and songs with an ambiguous "I" and an ambiguous "you." When I write "you" I mean "You, the reader." Why does a poet use "you" when they mean "Godzilla" or "Muhammad Ali"? This is not a mad lib. This is not online dating. This device is annoying.

10. Political poetry is not good. Nobody ever voted or changed their party affiliation because they read a poem. You are not on a soapbox. Twitter is not poetry.

Thank you

The author would like to thank: Alessi Laurent-Marke, Andrew Crane, Angel Ceballos, Ann DeJarnett, Andy Takakjian, Anton Newcombe, Barbara Frigo, Bev Davies, Bradley Dupray, Brian Jacobs, Bucky Sinister, Colin Newman, David Eggers, David Harding, Dee Madden, Donald Grose, Dot Allison, Eurydice Eve, Gail Eigl, Gayle Hutchens, Gene Brunak, Genesis P-Orridge, George Scrivani, Gil Fuhrer, Graham Lewis, Gregory Esposito, Jack Brewer, Jack Skelley, Jason Santos, Jeannie Daughtery, Kurt Lipschutz, Laura Markley, Lauren and Alan Marke, Leah Gualtieri, Liane Chan, Marilyn Johnson, Maw Shein Win, Michael Angelo Torres, Monica Welle, Nancy Gallo, Norma Cole, Rex Bruce, Robert Lanham, Russel Swensen, Stacy Lande, Stanley Gontarski, Steve Stultz, Susan Davis, Susan Whetstone, Suzanne Ramsey, Thomas Stolmar, Wendy Watson, and AJ Weiner.

Alexander Laurence was born in Los Angeles. He attended CSULB and San Francisco Art Institute. He has contributed to the books The Hipster Handbook (2004), Reefer Movie Madness (2010), Degenerative Prose (1995), and books about the history of Grove Press. He is also the author of a book of short stories: Five Fingers Make A Fist (2007). He presently works as a tour manager and has traveled the world with indie bands. He is the founder of the website The Portable Infinite, and has a weekly internet radio show New Noise on Radio KAJW.

www.ingramcontent.com/pod-product-compliance
Lightning Source LLC
Chambersburg PA
CBHW051507120626
46551CB00012B/810

* 9 7 8 1 9 5 8 6 6 1 0 2 4 *